Table of Contents

SECRETS OF HOME

WINE MAKING

BARRY NADEL

Text copyright©2016 Dr. Barry Nadel

All rights reserved

Agrosearch

Rehov HaSilo 9

Kfar Pines, Israel 37920

Publisher's Cataloging-in-Publication data

Nadel, Barry.

A title of a book: Secrets of Home Wine Making / Barry Nadel

ISBN 9798215292990

First Edition

I. INTRODUCTION

The secrets of home wine making is divided into two categories. The first concerns the physical properties of the wine. This is the more important of the two. One needs to produce technically sound wine. I define technically sound wine as wine that is clear, good color, and no off-tastes or odors. The second secret is the blending of varieties. This is all a matter of palate. Just like you can alter wine color by adding a small amount of wine from a teinturiers variety (varieties with very intense red color) you can make your wine more complex by blending various varieties together.

This book is unique for two reason: First, the approach to home wine making in this book is to help the wine makers to produce technologically sound wines. You can make good wine or bad wine from good grapes. Most of the problems are how to tweak the process to produce a clear, wine free of off-tastes and smells. Second, it provides a step-by-step method of how to produce different types of wine at home.

Winemaking has become a serious hobby in many homes throughout the world, but there are many misconceptions about it for those who want to join the hobby.

1. Homemade Wines are of Low Quality.

This is not true. Like any hobby the more you practice the better you are at accomplishing good results. Don't expect great results the first time. However, by following the steps in this book you can make a decent wine the first time.

1. Wine is Time Consuming. Isn't that the reason we want hobbies, to take up our time? Only the beginning is time consuming, harvesting, cleaning, crushing, and initiating the fermentation. Today there are many kits that reduce the time needed for the hobby.
2. Home Wine Making is Expensive.

This was true in the past if you wanted to make any amount of wine beyond 35 liters. There was a need for equipment that could cost, but unlike other hobbies that the materials are disposable, wine equipment can be used for decades.

1. The one of the objectives of this book is to prevent homemade wine from spoiling. It is a big complaint, but mostly caused by sloppy procedures. Take the time for proper sanitation, especially your storage vessels. If you maintain good procedure, the quality of your wine should be able to be maintained for years.

Wine can be simple or complex and as one's skills at winemaking improve, making a good wine becomes an art form. The winemaker's canvas is his bottle and his subject is color, aroma, and taste. One of the most important parts of making a good complex wine is producing a technically sound wine. Technically sound wine will have a good clear color, no strange foreign odors, and no off-tastes. There are numerous books published about wine, each one informative on one or more of the many diverse aspects surrounding wine and the processes making it. The intention of this booklet is to provide the public with an introduction into the world of wine and the specific practical information to make and enjoy homemade grape and fruit wines that will be technically sound.

There is a great number of books available on home winemaking. Most of them are full of beautiful pictures, sketches, and receipts on how to make wine. This book's intention is to not just to teach the how, but the why. This book intends to provide the public with the information to distinguish between poor and superior wines by their specific attributes (flavor, aroma, color, bouquet, and taste).

There are many types and styles of wine. Wine experts will inform us that this wine is better than that one or the aroma and taste of wine X produced by company A is superior to wine Y produced by Company B. This booklet will teach one how to sift through the information that is objective and that which is subjective. One critical fact one should always remember, taste as opposed to all the other attributes of wine, is one hundred percent subjective. Each individual has his or her likes and dislikes. When it comes to taste, do not depend on anyone else. Your tongue is the best judge of the matter. No matter how many experts tell you the wine is bad or not technically sound, if you like it then it's good for you. The likelihood of a wine that is not clear, has off-tastes or odors is enjoyable, is small.

Wine can be divided into many categories. Below is a simple system, easy to follow. For our purposes, grape wines can be divided into three general groups, natural, and dessert and appetizer wines. Below is a table categorizing the different wine types.

Wine Classification

.

Natural Wines and Dessert and Appetizer

9-14% Alcohol 15-21% Alcohol

1. Natural 2. Dessert and Appetizers

A. Still wines (no excess CO_2) A. Sweet wines

1) Dry Table wines 1. White-muscatel &

No noticeable sweetness 2. White port

a. white 2. Red- port & red

b. rose (pink) Muscat

c. red

These kinds of wines are in general B. Sherries (White-sweet

consumed with food. or dry wines that have

B. Slightly sweet table wines that have been oxidized

C. Sweet Table Wines purposely oxidized).

1) Whites l. baked

2) Red 2. aged

3) 'Old Wines' with added caramel 3. flor

D. Slightly gassy wines C. Flavored Specialty

1) White Wines

2) Red 1. Vermouth

E. Sparkling wines

(With large amounts of Co2 added)

1) Champagne (natural & bulk)

a) White

b) Pink

2) Artificially introduced CO2

3) Red-Sparkling burgundy

Natural wines are wines whose alcohol content is made one hundred percent by natural fermentation of grape sugar into alcohol by yeast. These wines alcohol and sugar content depend on how complete the fermentation took place. Wines of this type are consumed at meals or light foods, such as like dry white wines with apples and cheese. In Israel) most sweet wine is produced specifically for religious consumption, i.e., for *Kiddush* and *Havdalah*. There are also old wines. These are just sweet wines with caramel added to them to give them a slight musty taste and flavor, not at all imitating a truly aged wine.

Appetizer wines are drunk before meals as a prelude to the food. These wines have a slight amount of sweetness. They are wines drunk in the company of other people in small amounts while talking before a meal. Dessert wines are also of high alcohol content (15 to 21%). They are consumed after meals or with your dessert. They are consumed in small quantities.

Sparkling wines are wines which give off a continual flow of bubbles (CO2 gas) for an extended period (hours) after opening. Since natural champagnes are expensive, they are today associated with joyous occasions. True sparkling wines are produced by a secondary yeast fermentation in a closed container i.e., bottle or large vessel. Thus, the CO2 gas produced by the fermentation is trapped inside the wine and released upon exposure to air.

II. BIOLOGY OF GRAPES AND WINE.

The biology of wine making involves:

1) Grapes,

2) Yeast; wild and domestic and

3) Bacteria.

Grapes

In the past, most wines were made from the European grape species *Vitis vinifera*. There are over five thousand different cultivated varieties grown around the world. The variety of grape used for wine making will determine the color, aroma, acid content and flavor of the wine produced.

Grapes are long lived woody bushes, some over an 100 years old. Their growing season is from spring to fall, producing the fruit in clumps called clusters or bunches. The quality of grapes of any the variety depends on its genetic makeup, on environmental conditions in which it grew, on accumulative heat, wind, water supply, disease and insects, and the care the plants receive from the viticulturist. Most wine varieties produce higher quality grapes if grown under cool growing conditions in temperate latitudes or high altitudes. Warm to hot climates normally cause the grapes to be high in sugar and low in total acid, thus producing wines of 10-14% alcohol, but flat in taste. One must, therefore, not always buy grapes by their varietal name. It is necessary pay attention to the origin of the grapes and always to test the grapes for acid and sugar content even if it is by taste before buying.

Yeast.

———

Wild yeast is found naturally on grapes. The 'bloom' or light white coating on grapes is a mixture of different wild yeast and bacteria. They are very sensitive to SO2 (sulfide) and normally produce wines of 4 to 6% alcohol (unless natural conditions are altered). Natural fermentation can produce special flavors or off tastes and spoilage due to the bacteria associated with them. To produce a cleaner, more uniform flavor, it is preferable to use a pure culture of domesticated yeast.

Wine yeast or domesticated yeast (*Saccharomyces cerevisiae,*) is also found on grapes but in much fewer numbers. Wine yeast are facultative anaerobes (no alcohol is produced if one hundred percent aerobic). They are more tolerant to alcohol and SO2 than the wild varieties. Many strains have been selected over the years for different fermentation rates, but the flavor differences are small. Other yeast species such as S. fermentii or S. bayanus are important in flor sherry and other specialty wines.

Like all living things, yeast require basic elements for growth:

1) Readily metabolized source of carbohydrate (i.e., sucrose, glucose, fructose, but not starch),

2) minerals-nitrogen source, phosphorus, and potassium,

3) Trace elements and

4) Vitamins.

Grape juice provides all the factors yeast need to grow, divide and convert sugar to alcohol. Many other fruit juices do not contain all these essential factors and, therefore, are more difficult to ferment.

Unlike many other microorganisms, wine yeast thrives in acid solutions, like grape juice (pH 3.2 to 4.5). This was important in the past because no human pathogens can grow in wine even if they were deliberately put in. Therefore, mixing wine with the polluted water was a way of producing safe drinking the water.

Bacteria

Acetobacter aceti or the acetic acid bacteria are the bacteria that convert your homemade wine into homemade vinegar. A. aceti converts alcohol into acetic acid, which in dilute amounts is called vinegar. Bacteria are ubiquitous and naturally occurring with grapes. They are obligate aerobes (i.e., they must have air to grow) and are very sensitive to SO_2. Bacteria are also inhibited by high alcohol (>14% by volume).

Lactobacillus or the lactic acid bacteria convert malic acid to lactic acid + CO_2. This fermentation is referred to as malo-lactic fermentation. A malo-lactic fermentation lowers the total acid content and raises the pH of the wine. This is desirable in high acid wines and in the production of many fruit wines.

Lactobacillus is anaerobic (not needing air to survive).

III. FERMENTAION CHEMISTRY

Before science played a role in fermentation science fermentation, people considered failed to realize the foaming, frothing, churning or boiling of the must as giving off heat. Today fermentation is defined as chemical changes brought about by microorganisms (i.e., yeast, bacteria, fungi) to various organic substances. An important commercial example would be the aerobic fermentation for the production of antibiotics. There are also anaerobic fermentations used in the food industry to produce pickled products, such as olives, pickled cucumber, and sauerkraut.

The simple overall equation of fermentation was formulated in 1810 by Gay-Lussac as 1 molecule of sugar being converted into 2 molecules of ethanol and 2 molecules of CO_2 or

$$\rightarrow 1 \text{ glucose } (C_6H_{12}O_6) \; 2 \text{ ethanol } (2C_2H_5OH) + 2\, CO_2 +$$

Approximately 56 kilocalories of energy (given off as heat). Why should all this chemical mumbo jumbo be at all of any interest to the home winemaker? If one pays attention to the last two facts in the equation, we discover the necessity of learning this formula.

Fermentation releases large amounts of CO_2 gas. In large wineries this has proven fatal more than once when people too close to a vigorously fermenting vat of wine were asphyxiated (suffocated). The CO_2 is given off at such a high rate it looks like the wine is boiling. This is important to the home winemaker. He must choose a fermenting vessel at least 25% larger than the amount of wine one wants to ferment, to prevent the fermenting must from spilling out of the vessel. The chance of affixation at home is about zero. Therefore, the active fermentation of grape juice (or other substrate) wine should be conducted in a well-aerated place.

Fresh grape juice comprises 70 to 80% water, and many dissolved solids. The soluble solids are composed of many organic and inorganic compounds. The compounds important to winemaking include:

1. sugars

2. organic acids

3. phenolic compounds

4. nitrogenous compounds

5. aroma compounds

6. minerals

7. pectic substances

Juice also contains contain insoluble substances as well. Some of these insoluble components are important to wine quality and it is only during and after fermentation that they become available to wine because they are soluble in alcohol.

The second important factor is the heat that is given off. If a fermentation reaches 37°C, the heat will kill the yeast. This is known as a 'stuck' fermentation. The addition of new yeast will restart the fermentation. Therefore, it is essential for good wine management to include a means to control the temperature of the fermentation.

IV. WINE AS ALCOHOL

———

It is of utmost importance to treat wine with respect and moderation. Of all the known alcohols in the world, only ethanol is least poisonous to human beings. All the other alcohols cause grievous bodily damage, some even in minute amounts. Excess wine is poisonous to our bodies.

Wine, however, consumed wisely in moderation, it can be both enjoyable and healthful.

The physiology of Alcohol in the human system

1) Alcohol acts as a depressant on the central nervous system. Wine acts as a 'stimulant' only by removing our inhibitions.

2) The absorption rapid and complete. It is absorbed more rapidly with the addition carbon dioxide. This is the reason that sparkling wines make you drunk faster. Its effect on the body is controlled by the amount of food in your digestive system and your body weight.

.

3) Wine alcohol is rapidly absorbed into all body fluids and its execration (via urine) is minimal.

4) Alcohol is metabolized in our system by the liver. The maximum amount of alcohol the liver can metabolize in a 24-hour period is 200~300 ml. High wine consumption leads to loss of appetite (and all the problems involved with it) and serious liver disease (Cirrhosis of the liver, which is fibrous scarring of the internal structure of the liver).

If it seems, I have dwelt overlong on over indulgence of wine (alcoholism); it is because of the seriousness of the problem which is increasing in throughout the world. It is not just a personal problem, but a major social problem in many parts of the world. Worldwide each year thousands of people are killed by drunk drivers. Let us all take advice from our teacher and sage King Solomon from his Proverbs Chapter 23:20. "Be not among Winebibbers; among gluttonous coffers of meat; for the drunkard and the glutton shall come to poverty: and drowsiness shall clothe a man with rag."

V. GRAPES

The first thing the home winemaker must know about grapes is that only good grapes can make good wine. It is impossible to make a superior wine, both technically and aesthetically, from bad grapes. There are two types of grapes grown: table grapes, those used for fruit and making raisins and wine grapes, used for making wine and brandy.

Figure 1, Anatomy of a grapevine

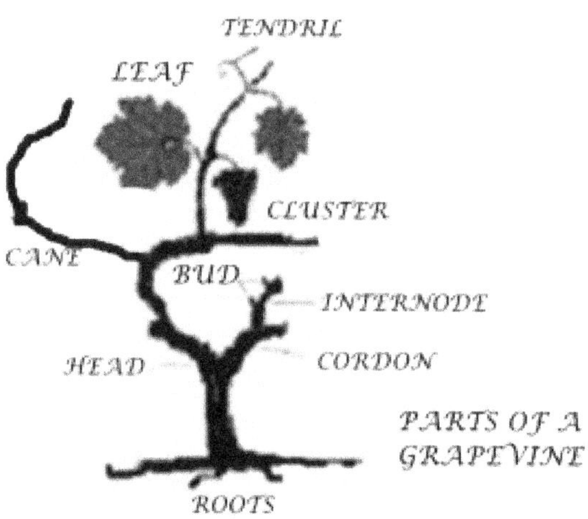

Table grapes (grapes for the fresh market) are large, high in soluble solids (fleshy), low in juice and total acid. They are picked at 14-1 8°Brix. Degrees of Brix is the standard measurement of the total soluble solids in a fluid. In grapes the sugar content of the juice makes up the vast majority of total soluble solids. They have a low ratio of skin surface to juice content.

Wine grapes are small, low in soluble solids, very juicy and higher in total acidity. They have a high skin surface to juice ratio, which for red wines are important for color extraction. Wine grapes are picked at 20 to 25° Brix.

Most wine grape varieties have white juice whether they are white or red varieties. There are special varieties which have red juice. They are varieties that can produce anthocyanins not only in the cells of the skin, but also in the cells of the flesh. These special varieties are called teinturiers. Examples of teinturiers are Alecante Bouchet, Royalty and Rubired. It is possible to produce a light rose-colored wine from these by fermenting the juice without the skins. Rose-colored wines can also be produced by fermenting red varieties for only one to two days on their skins.

BARRY NADEL

Figure 2: Grape Cluster Anatomy

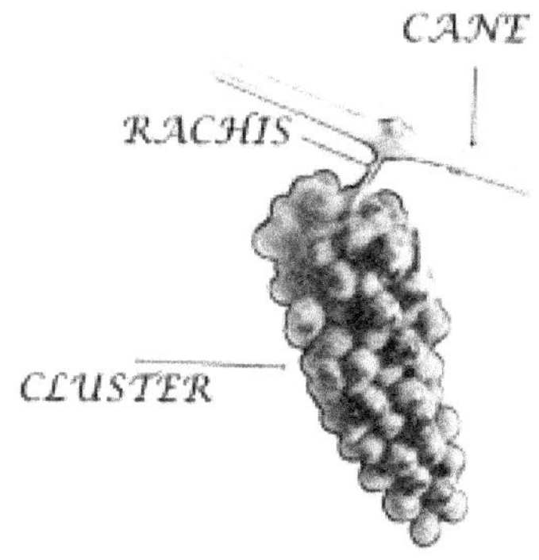

Characteristics

Below, I summarize important viticultural characteristics important to the home winemaker.

Viticultural Characteristics Important to Winemaking

White wine Harvest Taste Yields Cluster

size

Varieties

Chenin

Blanc early-mid* N** med-high large

French

Colombard early S-D high large

SAUVIGNON

Blanc mid D medium small

Semillon mid M med med-large

Emerald

Riesling early-mid D high med-large

Muscat

Canelli early D low medium

Red Wine

Varieties

Royalty mid S high medium

Rubired mid S high medium

Cabernet

Sauvignon late D low medium

Carignane late S large med-large

Grenache mid S large large

Petite

Sarah mid D large medium

Pinot

noir early D low small

* Mid =middle season.

D = distinctive, M= moderate, S= slightly distinctive and N= neutral.

Why Varietal Wine Grapes?

The concept of a good wine is easy to define technically, but impossible to define for individual tastes. It is possible, however, to know that one varietal wine (wine made predominately from one particular variety) is better than another.

Each individual wine grape variety has its own unique taste (or lack of it) and aroma as seen in the table above. In a blind test, an experienced wine taster has the ability to identify a particular wine is based on those distinct flavors and aromas. This unique flavor and aroma may be reduced by factors like:

1) Poor quality grapes,

2) Diluting a. making the wine from 2 or more varieties or b. blending in more than 30% of another wine and

3) The addition of sugar, which will obscure the varietal flavor.

Sugar has a physiological effect on our taste buds. When sugar is present with other tastes, our taste buds absorb the sugar taste more than any other flavor, thus masking any unique varietal flavor that might have been present. This is one reason experience wine drinkers prefer dry wines, i.e., to experience the unique taste of the wine. There is just one type of table wine in which it is desirable to leave residual sugar, i.e., Muscat. When Muscat is fermented to complete dryness it has a harsh, unpleasant bitter taste.

The quality of a unique varietal taste depends on the quality of the grapes and of the winemaker. If the wine maker wants to produce a wine with a pronounced varietal flavor, he must use at least 30% of his grapes from the particular variety he plans to make the wine from. I personally recommend that the home winemaker to use at least 90% of the varietal grape he or she chooses. Most blending is done for economic reasons. A bottle of wine labeled as being of a particular variety receives 50-200% more money than a generically labeled bottle. This makes it is economically worthwhile in the short run to use the legal minimum (51%).

How the Home Winemaker Selects Good Wine Grapes

1) Sugar Content. Any good viticulturist will have a refractometer for determining sugar content. Select grapes at random from individual clusters and vines (or from containers already picked). Pick 4~8 berries at random from 10 to 15 different clusters. Crush all the berries together and place a sample on the refractometer, which gives its readings in Brix. For wine between 11-13% alcohol, you want grapes between 20-23° Brix.

.Acid Content (2

The best criterion for selecting grapes is their sugar-acid ratio. This cannot be done analytically by most home winemakers, as it requires special equipment. The next best thing is an organoleptic test (acting on or involving the use of the senses of taste and smell). Place a small sample of the juice in your mouth. Don't swallow it! The excess sugar will lower your ability to test further samples. Swish the sample around the inside of your mouth and then spit it out. Then rinse your mouth with water. The aim is to get a rough estimation of the total acidity. If the taste is flat, then the resultant wine will be flat. It is possible to buy tartaric acid and added it to your fermenting must. Another home solution is to add to your crushed grapes, 10-15% less ripe or greenish grapes (which will be higher in acid).

3) Physical Quality of the grapes. Closely examine the grapes for debris, contamination, and insect damage. All these can cause off tastes and had odors in your wine.

4) Time of Harvest.

Pick your grapes at the coolest time of the day. The temperature of the grape juice influences the rate of fermentation. Grapes picked during the heat of the day will have a higher temperature and will require more energy to cool them down to enable a controlled fermentation.

Seasonal Strategy:

If you plan to make several wines in one season, pay special attention to their ripening dates. There are two important reasons. First, most home winemakers lack space to ferment more than one wine at a time. Therefore, select varieties that will allow you time to finish each operation with little overlapping. Try to maintain at least three weeks between each new batch. The second reason is grapes that are picked too late in their season will be high in sugar and low in acid. This will produce a high alcohol wine that is whose taste is flat.

Picking Grapes, Yourself

Always pick grapes very early in the morning: 5-7:30 a.m. This ensures that the grapes will be cool and this will help in the initial control of the temperature of the fermentation. If you are picking the grapes yourself, as mentioned above, try to include 8-10% unripe clusters. These should be fermented separately and use later for blending if you suspect the wine will be low in acid. By using the same variety of grapes you prevent dilution of your variety flavors and aromas. The standard method is to add tartaric acid to adjust the total acid content or pH.

FIGURE 3. HAND HARVESTING grapes.

VI. HOME WINE MAKING OPERATIONS

The operations involved in home winemaking parallel exactly those of commercial operations except on a much smaller scale. Below is a list of all the steps involved in making home wine.

1. Analysis of the Grapes, sugar-acid ratio, and damage to the grapes (from birds, insects or disease).
2. Preparing the Grapes for Fermentation: harvest, crush and destem.
3. Sulfuring.

4. Fluid Recovery and pressing.

5. Fermentation-natural vs. induced,

6. Transfer and racking.

7. Special operations-addition of spirits or sugar and pH adjustment.

8. Tartrate Stabilization-removal of excess Potassium bitartrate crystals.

9. Aging-glass, wood, stainless steel.

10. Clarification, sedimentation and fining.

11. Blending.

12. Bottling

Each phase of the wine-making process and the necessary equipment will be explained below.

1. Analysis of Grapes

The first step, choosing grapes, will be skipped since it has already been discussed in the previous section. Remember to have a small hand pruning shears to remove any diseased or damaged grapes from the clusters. Insects can hide between and on the grapes inside the cluster. Wash the grapes and allow the excess water to drain off before crushing.

Figure 6. Mealy bug infected cluster

The two of the most important factors for determining the time to harvest are sugar and acid. As grapes ripen their sugar levels will increase, while acids will decrease to a manageable level. The trick is to harvest your grapes when you have sufficient sugar for a good fermentation and enough acid so the wine won't be flat. Contingent on the variety you grow or that you are using for wine making, the optimal sugar and acid levels will vary.

B

Harvest

.(elow is a list of optimal Sugar-Acid-pH ratios (TA=Total Acid

Variety pH °Brix TA Final pH

Dry Red Wines

Cabernet

Sauvignon 3.3-3.4 24-26.5 .6-.7 3.6-3.7

Merlot: 3.2-3.4 23-25.5 .65-.8 3.55-3.65

Cabernet

Franc: 3.2-3.4 23-25.5 .65-.8 3.55-3.6

Malbec: 3.2-3.4 23-26 .65-.8 3.55-3.6

Pinot

Noir: 3.2-3.3 22-25. .65-.8 3.5-3.55

Zinfandel: 3.3-3.45 24-28 .6-.75 3.65-3.75

GRENACHE: 3.3-3.45 25-27 .6-.75 3.65-3.75

Petite

Sirah: 3.3-3.5 25-27 .6-.7 3.6-3.75

Tempranillo: 3.3-3.5 24-27 .6-.7 3.65-3.8

Sangiovese: 3.2-3.4 23-26 .6-.75 3.65-3.8

Target Values for White Wines, Native Wines, and Rosé

Riesling: 2.9-3.2 20-24 .7-.9 3.1-3.4

Gewurztraminer:

2.9-3.2 20-24 .7-.9 3.2-3.4

Sauvignon

Blanc: 2.9-3.3 20-24 .7-.9 3.2-3.4

Pinot

Griggio: 2.9-3.2 20-24 .7-.9 3.2-3.4

Chardonnay:

3.0-3.3 22-25 .7-.9 3.3-3.45

Concord:

2.9-3.3 14-19 .8-1 3.2-3.45

Niagara:

2.9-3.3 14-18 .8-1 3.2-3.45

Rosé:

2.9-3.3 18-23 .7-.1 3.2-3.5

2. Preparing the Grapes for Fermentation

ONCE YOU HAVE HARVESTED the grapes, the next step is to crush and prepare them for fermentation. It is important to know when the grapes were last sprayed and with what pesticide. It may be necessary to wash the grapes before use if they had been recently sprayed with a long-lasting pesticide. Your crush should be done in a place close to where your fermentation will be carried out. There should be sufficient room and water accessible for cleaning up afterwards. The easiest and most ancient method of crushing grapes (in small amounts) is with your feet. Wash your feet well before crushing. One can crush by hand, but it is not feasible for more than 8 kg of grapes. It is physically very difficult and tiring work. There are small electrical and hand driven Crushers available to the home winemaker. These items are available in any shop that sells equipment for winemaking.

Figure 7. Home grape crushing equipment

The vessel in which you crush your grapes should be at least 10 cm deep. It shouldn't be too large as to make it difficult to transfer to your fermenting vat. You may use any stainless steel, wood (waterproof) or food grape plastic containers. Avoid copper, zinc, tin and bronze vessels, as they give off heavy metals that can be poisonous to the consumer or detrimental to the wine. The next important operation is to destem the crush grapes, Remove all the stems and leaves from the crushed grapes. This is done immediately after each batch of grapes that are crushed. Run your hands through the crushed mixture, catching the stems between your fingers. Have a garbage can handy for immediate disposal. Stems covered in grapes juice readily attract flies and other insects. Stems and leaves give a grassy taste to the wine and add excessive tannins. Tannins are one factor that give the harsh flavor to wine.

3. Sulfuring

Sulfur as sulfur dioxide (SO_2) can be used in two different stages of the wine-making process. First, it can be added immediately after crush to kill all the naturally occurring microorganisms (yeast and bacteria) and to act as an antioxidant and/or be added at the end of the fermentation for the same reasons.

Air, i.e., oxygen, is wine's no. one enemy. Exposure to air causes a chemical reaction known as oxidation. This oxidation may be induced by enzymes in the fruit or by direct reaction between phenolic compounds in the must, and oxygen from air. Sulfur dioxide reduces the oxidation-reduction potential of the juice or wine. Sulfur dioxide is a strong enough reducing agent that is oxidized in preference to the phenolic compounds in the must. Only free sulfur dioxide is reactive. Therefore, the ratio between bound and free sulfur dioxide is important. The amount of free sulfur dioxide depends on temperature, amount of sugar, aldehyde and the pH of the juice or wine. This oxidation causes the burned-like taste and turns the wine a brown color. This is particularly bad for white wines, but in some red wines it is encouraged (port). Sulfur can be added in many forms, but the most available to the home winemaker is potassium meta-bisulfate. It is available as a powder and can be added directly into the grape juice. Make sure the SO_2 is thoroughly mixed into the must. The amount of free (active) SO_2 available from

Potassium meta-bisulfate is 50%. Therefore, if 100 ppm (ppm = parts per million) of SO_2 is required you need to add 200 ppm of K-meta-bisulfate. The normal range of SO_2; in wine is 75-150 ppm, where the upper range is used for particularly spoiled grapes or wine that may suffer excessive exposure to air. Be exceedingly careful with the addition of SO_2 because an excess causes the wine to have a burned match smell.

If you want a natural fermentation, do not add SO_2 because it will kill all the natural yeast. However, if you plan to inoculate with a pure culture of domesticated yeast, it is essential to kill off the entire wild micro flora, so they won't compete with the domesticated yeast. One should wait two to three hours after adding SO2 before adding the domesticated yeast culture. The amount of potassium meta-bisulfate needed for 10 liters of must is shown in the table below.

Amounts of Sulfur Dioxide to Add to Musts

Maturity of Grapes condition ppm equivalent in teaspoons

Under ripeClean 75 1/3

Mature Clean 100 1/2

Overripe Moldy 125 3/5

If you have a scale available, it is preferable to use exact measurements as to avoid excessive amounts.

After fermentation has finished, the addition of sulfur dioxide is recommended for all wines. It is crucial not to add too much SO2 since it causes an unpleasant odor. Adding between 75 to 125 ppm is recommended depending on the condition of the wine. SO2 gives lasting protection against enzymatic oxidation, but little against non-enzymatic oxidation (due to slow exposure to air(, and therefore, does not interfere with the aging process.

Sorbic acid is used both instead of and in conjunction with sulfur dioxide. It is very effective in preventing malo-lactic fermentation in wine is in storage. Sorbic acid excess will also produce unpleasant odors. Control of yeast growth in sweet table wines can be obtained by using 80 ppm sorbic acid and 30 ppm of SO2 together. Its sensory threshold is around 135 ppm, but some people are sensitive to it as low as 50 ppm. Therefore, the recommended dosage of sorbic acid and sulfur dioxide together should not exceed 125 ppm. Sorbic acid itself should not exceed 90 ppm and should not be less than 70 ppm.

Fumaric acid is also used to prevent malo-lactic fermentation. Fumaric acid at the rate of 1.5gm/Liter with 75 ppm SO2 has been found to be very effective as an antiseptic. Using fumaric acid also increases the total titratable acid.

4 Fluid Recovery:

———

Here, it will be necessary to define several terms to understand the following processes.

a) The term must refers to both the solution of crushed grapes to be fermented and the fermenting solution itself. The term wine is used for the liquid upon completion of fermentation.

In white wines, must is the grapes juice after pressing and in red wines must is the mixture of juice, skins, and seeds.

b) Pomace is the solid waste material remaining after pressing. The pressing causes it to be in the form of cakes. It contains all the skins, stems, seeds and debris.

c) Free Run is the must that exists from the crush without pressing. This is often fermented separately in high-quality wineries. Pressing releases many more materials (such as tannins, which add harshness) which would not be found in the free run.

A ton of grapes yields from 550 to 700 liters of juice with an average of around 640 liters. Dry pomace averages about 5% of the total weight. The efficiency of the total yield of must depends upon the variety in question and on how the must is pressed from the skins. For small amounts of wine, it suffices to place 2 to 3 kg of must in 2 to 4 layers of gauze and squeeze out the must. For large amounts of wine (over 100 liters), it is advisable to use a press. It is important to have a means of waste disposal available, because like the stems, pomace quickly attracts insects.

Figure 8. Fluid recovery of must from crushed grapes.

5. Fermentation:

Fermentation is the conversion of sugar to alcohol (ethanol) by yeast. In the process (as mentioned above) CO_2 and heat are given off. The control of this heat is essential in winemaking. Temperature is the prime control of the rate of fermentation. White wines need low temperatures (8 to 14°C) to retain good aroma and flavors. White wines ferment much longer than red wines. Red wines can be fermented at 20 to 30°C depending on the variety. Once the temperature reaches 37°C it kills the yeast and the fermentation stops. This is known as a `stuck' fermentation and can be restarted by allowing the must to cool and the addition of a pure yeast starter. During fermentation, the temperature rises 1 to 1.25°C for every drop of 1° Brix.

For example, if we start with grapes of 24° Brix at a temperature of 25°C. The fermentation of 24° Brix will produce 24 to 32° of heat. It is obvious from the calculation that one reaches 37°C and a stuck fermentation.

How to control fermentation temperature? For white wines, which are fermented without skins, the temperature of the fermentation can be control by various types of refrigeration of either the vessel or the entire area of the fermentation. This is generally difficult for the home winemaker to do and is one reason I recommend only those people with proper equipment to make white wines at home. Small amounts of white wine can be fermented in your home refrigerator. Ferment during the day inside the refrigerator and in the evening when the temperature has fallen to 14°C, allow the must to ferment outside till the morning. This is not ideal but passable. If an old refrigerator is available, that can be adjusted to 8 to 14°C, it would be the best situation, but still only a maximum of 40 liters can be produced.

Red wines are much easier for the home winemaker to handle. Initial fermentation may take place in open. One should use containers which allow the generated heat to escape. Red wines are initially fermented with the skins to extract the color. The skins, seeds, and stems create the components of the cap. This cap acts as an efficient insulator, which captures most of the heat and a portion of the CO2. Managing the cap is, therefore, the key to temperature control of red wines. The cap should be broken up and mixed back into the fermenting must at least two, preferably three times a day, morning and evening. This breaks up the insulating action allowing the heat to escape. Breaking the cap provides better skin contact for the extraction of color. This is done by punching down the cap and mixing the cap back into the must, stirring it with a stick about 20% longer than the vessel is deep. In commercial wineries this is done by pumping the must from beneath the cap and spraying the wine over the cap.

Figure 9. Fermentation in Plastic Vessel

Table wines fermented to complete dryness will produce alcohol at a rate of 0.55% alcohol for every degree Brix. Example: must which starts at 24° Brix will produce a wine of 13.2% alcohol. With this conversion rate, you can pick (or buy) your grapes to produce the exact amount of alcohol you desire.

Fermentation should always be carried out on a platform to ensure ease of transferring of the wine (by gravitation) in later operations. Fermentation can be accomplished in any food-grade container large enough so it is not more than ½ to 3/4 full. This prevents must from spilling out when it is actively fermenting.

There are three basic types of fermentation they are:

A) Natural

b) Controlled

C) Maceration Carbonique.

a) Natural Fermentation.

The 'bloom' or the light whitish powder found on all grapes is a mixture of wild yeast and bacteria. These indigenous yeasts can ferment grape must. The procedure is simple, Crush the grapes and allow the natural yeast population to increase and conduct the fermentation. Natural fermentation takes a few days longer to conduct since active fermentation does not occur until the yeast population has increased to a sufficient number. This is the oldest and simplest method of making wine and technically for quality control the poorest. First, since no SO_2 is added there is no protection against bacterial fermentation which can produce off tastes, foul odors, and potentially dangerous chemicals. Second, there is oxidation, which is of a greater risk in natural fermentation, because of the time lapse till active fermentation. The problem of oxidation can be in part overcome by adding 5 to 10% active starter from an ongoing natural fermentation, but there will be oxidation damage to the starter.

Third, wild yeast rarely ferments to above 5% alcohol. This leaves the wines open to secondary fermentations, mostly malo-lactic, which will lower the acid content of the wine and the lack of acid is already a general problem in Israeli wines. The fourth problem is taste and aroma. With wild yeast, there is no control over the unique tastes and aromas which might develop. They may range from uniquely unusual and pleasant, to bad smelling and undrinkable. Natural fermentation is easiest, but least dependable method.

B. Controlled Fermentation.

Controlled fermentation by definition is a fermentation regulated and manipulated by man, in our case to produce a uniform reproducible product called wine.

Step 1. Remove all diseased and spoiled grapes.

Step 2. Crush and destem the grapes.

Step 3. Add 75 to 120 ppm SO_2, in whatever form you prefer. For white wines, whose grapes are in good condition do not add more than 100 ppm SO_2. For red wine add 75 to 100 ppm SO_2. Only use high dosages of SO_2 if there are a lot of contaminated grapes. Remember, however, excessive SO_2 causes the 'burned match' smell.

Step 4. Wait 1- to 1.5 hours before adding pure yeast starter. Yeast starter is made by adding a culture of pure wine yeast to a liter of fresh squeezed grape juice. Once it ferments it's used to inoculate ten liters of grape juice, until you have between 3 to 5% of the total amount of wine, you will be making. It is preferable to make the starter from the same variety you will ferment or some neutral variety like Sultanina. This should all be started 2 to 3 weeks before your planned fermentation. Initial active fermentation can take place in an open vessel.

.

Step 5. After 8 to 12 days (for refrigerated fermentations, it will be longer) transfer the fermenting must into a closed container with an air look.

Step 6. When fermentation has finished (no more bubbles are evident in the airlock) add more SO_2 at a rate of 70 to 100 ppm. The amount added depends on how well one can minimize air contact. If you have proper equipment and work fast, then don't add more than 85 ppm SO_2, if not use around 100 ppm.

C. *Maceration Carbonique*

Step 1 In *maceration carbonique* (recommended only for red wines) the whole berries are place in a closed container, the fermenting vessel, and brought under anaerobic conditions, i.e., fermentation takes place in the absence of air. This is achieved by sealing the fermenting vessel hermetically. Under these conditions, the fruit's metabolism is changed from aerobic to anaerobic and fermentation is started inside the skins. This should be allowed to continue for 8-10 days until the must has reached 4 to 5% alcohol.

Step 2 Prepare 3 to 5% pure yeast starter, so it will be ready at the end of the 10 days of anaerobic fermentation.

Step 3 After 8 to 10 days of anaerobic fermentation, crush, destem and press the grapes.

Step 4 Add 75 to 120 ppm SO_2 and wait 2 to 3 hours.

Step 5 Add the actively fermenting pure wine yeast starter to the must.

The rest of the procedures are identical to those in a controlled fermentation.

The process of *maceration carbonique* produces wines with the following characteristics:

a) Fresh fruity taste,

b) Low tannins,

c) A unique flavor as compared to a regular

fermentation and

d) Short-lived wines.

The flavor of these wines deteriorates after 18 months. This method of fermentation is recommended for wine, which will not be aged and drunk within 10 months of bottling.

6. Transfer and Racking

The next major operation after fermentation is transferring and separating the wine from all the solid particles suspended in it. This process is called racking. Its purpose is to remove all dead yeast, seeds, pieces of stems and assorted floating solid particles.

Step 1 With the completion of fermentation the wine is allowed to settle by gravitation for 8 to 10 days.

Step 2 As the wine settles one will observe a thick layer of mud-like material begin to collect at the bottom of the vessel. This material is known as lees. This comprises all the solid particles mentioned above. A food-grade plastic hose can now be inserted into the closed container and the clear wine siphoned off, leaving behind the lees. This process may need to be repeated 2 to 4 times. Each time you need to allow for successively longer time ranging from three to six weeks.

Now it is essential that the home winemaker have as many sized bottles or containers available. For each time you rack the wine, the total amount of wine left is less and therefore if left in the same containers there will damage due to oxidation (exposure to air). Always keep the vessels holding the wine full and sealed as tight as possible.

7. Special Operations.

At this stage of the wine-making process, one begins many of the chemical manipulations. Each operation will be discussed, and the methodology explained.

a) Addition sugar: Sugar can be added at this stage for two reasons:

1) For sweetening wines that have fermented to dryness and

2) For starting a secondary yeast fermentation (in the bottle or bulk) for producing sparkling wines.

This will be discussed in the section on sparkling wines.

It is important for the home winemaker to use wines of high alcohol content 13 to 15% as to avoid unwanted secondary fermentation in the bottle. Low alcohol wines with residual sugar can be preserved by sterile filtration, which is not available to the vast majority of home winemakers. Using overripe grapes to make sweet wine does not always produce the desired effect. The sweetness of your wine is an individual matter of taste. Therefore, each individual winemaker must adjust the amount of sugar empirically until the desired result is achieved.

Dissolve sugar in a small volume of wine and then add the mixture back into the bulk of the wine. Mix thoroughly and then sample the wine. Repeat this as many times as necessary. There is no way to reverse this procedure. It is, therefore, recommended that about 10% of the wine should be kept aside till you are sure you have reached the desired level of sweetness. If you should exceed the desired level, you will have the 10% with which to dilute the sweetness back down.

One can also buy a residual sugar home test kit. This simple test kit will give you an accurate reading of your sugar content in your wine.

b) Dilution: For home winemakers who desire a lower alcohol wine and don't mind losing some taste, they can add water to the wine to reduce the alcohol content. This is not legal for commercial enterprises. If you want to dilute the wine use filtered, bacteria-free, or sterile boiled water. This caution is necessary because with the reduced alcohol content the wine is more susceptible to unwanted secondary fermentations and contaminations.

C) Addition of Acid: In warm areas, like California, Israel, Australia, and South Africa, most of the European varieties bred for the northern climates produce high acid wines. In colder regions should as all of northern and central Europe, northeastern United States the wines can be flat without sufficient acid. Technically sound wine should have a good acid balance according to the characteristics of the variety.

Low acid wines, flat tasting, can be caused by the lack of acid in the grapes or by secondary malo-lactic fermentation. Total acid content is easy to conduct at home and for the serious home winemaker it is worthwhile to invest in the small amount of equipment and chemicals needed.

Today there are simple wine acid test kits with simple instructions.

Figure 10. Home Wine Acid Test Kit.

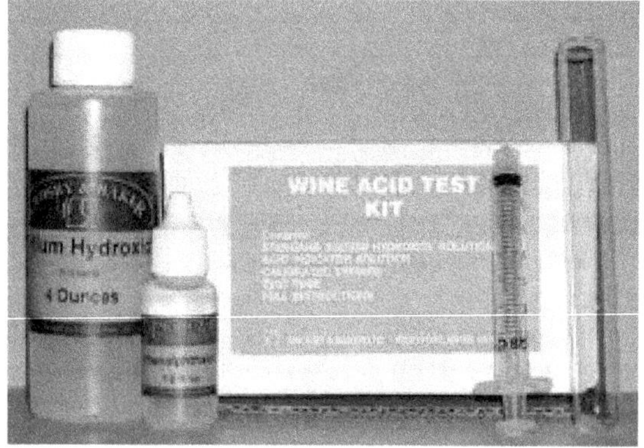

However, if one doesn't want to invest in the equipment and/or kits, then one must test organoleptically and make adjustments.

The acid most used for altering the acidic component of your wine is tartaric acid. Citric and malic acid can be used but are less successful. Tartaric acid is readily available from your local wine supply store.

Below is a table which provides guidelines for the amount of acid needed to produce a well-balanced wine. The amounts are given in the percent of titratable acid as tartaric acid.

Recommended Acid Content for Different Wines

<u>Wine Types Acid Content</u>

Red 0.6-0.9%

Rose 0.7-0.9%

White 08.-1.0%

Dessert 0.4-0.65%

Sparkling Wines 0.7-1.0%

ONE OF MY PERSONAL secrets is to use a natural substitute. As grapes ripen, their acid content drops. Harvest 8-10% of your total harvest at 16° Brix when the grapes still have a high acid content and ferment this separately. When you reach the above-mentioned stage determine how much of the high acid wine you want to blend in by adding a small amount at a time. The advantage of this system is that you are adding a hundred percent natural source of acid along with its varietal flavors and aromas. It is preferable to use the same variety that you are fermenting to prevent dilution of the varietal flavors and aromas.

If you should by accident add too much acid, all is not lost. $CaCO_3$, calcium carbonate, is excellent for -removing tartaric acid from wine. It works so well you must use this product with great care as not to remove too much acid. Add the calcium carbonate and mix the wine thoroughly. It will slowly settle to the bottom as calcium tartrate. Allow the wine to settle for 10-14 days and then rack the clear wine off the accumulated on the bottom of the vessel.

d) pH:

The pH is a scale of 1-12 for measuring the amount of acid or base in a solution. The lower end of the scale being 1 to 7 is progressively less acid (H+) until you hit neutral at pH 7. The upper end of the scale, 7-12, is being progressively more basic (OH-). pH is very important to home winemakers.

The reasons are:

1) A low pH (acid) adds bacterial resistance to the wine, since bacteria cannot grow well below a pH of 4 or below.

2) The pH of the wine controls the amount of free sulfur dioxide. The lower the pH, the freer SO_2 there is available. Some authorities don't recommend the addition of SO_2 for musts with a pH below 3.1

3) The tint of the color is affected especially in red wines and

4) pH plays an important role in the acid taste and sourness of the wine. The pH of most wines range between 3-3.8. Table wines should have a pH of less than 3.5 and dessert wines less than 3.8. Wines with a pH of less than 3.4 have better resistance to spoilage, taste fresher, and fruiter and have a better shade of color.

The test for pH is by far the simplest. There is a special paper called Litmus paper that changes color when place into a solution. The color depends on the solutions pH. It is available from almost all firms who supply biological equipment and chemicals. Clear directions are given in each package and they are all provided with a scale. I recommend two sets of test papers, one general, with a range of 1-7 and one specific with a range of 3 to 4. The pH of a must can be adjusted downward (made acidic) with the addition of tartaric acid.

Example: To adjust the pH of a must from 3.6 to 3.4 one needs about 43 grams tartaric acid to 10 liters of must or wine. To raise the pH of a low pH wine or must, add calcium carbonate (see use of calcium carbonate above).

e) Addition of alcohol: If one wants to produce dessert wines, this is the stage to add the wine spirits to the wine. The alcohol content of dessert wines ranges from 15 to 13%. Exact details and calculations will be discussed in the section on dessert wines.

8 Tartrate Stabilization:

Grape juice is high in tartaric acid and potassium. As the juice is converted into alcohol, the wine becomes a supersaturated solution of potassium tartrate (cream of tartar). Sand-like potassium bitartrate crystals form in the wine and gravitate to the bottom of the wine vessel. The result is unpleasant for anyone drinking the wine (no one likes sand in their wine).

Wine, while still in bulk containers should be stabilized for excess K-bitartrate. The procedure is simple but difficult for the home winemaker. In commercial wineries the temperature of the wine is reduced to -4 to -5 "C and held at that temperature for 10 to 14 days. At home, without special equipment, it is possible to stabilize the wine in the refrigerator in small lots of 5 to 10 liters. Keep the wine refrigerated until you see the excess k-bitartrate precipitate at the bottom of the vessel. Then rack off the clear wine off the crystals. Another method can be used if the wine will not be stored for more than 10 to 15 months. Rack the wine before bottling and if the wine is not subjected to very cold temperatures it should hold for 10 to 15 months. These crystals can be purified (consult the Merck Index) and used the following season as tartaric acid.

9. Aging:

The purpose of aging is to mellow the harsh tastes of red wines. There are several varieties, when young, have a high content of tannins. Very slow aging causes the tannins to oxidate and reduce the harshness.

One method of controlling a slow oxidation is by aging the wine in wooden barrels. The aging of wine is conducted in oak barrels or in corked bottles. In large commercial enterprises, large glass-lined containers are sometimes used. Aging in oak adds a vanilla like taste to the wine. As a general principle, white and rose wines are not aged in wood. Not all red wines improve with wood aging either. Among the leading wines that are commonly aged in wood are Ruby Cabernet, Cabernet Sauvignon, Merlot, Petite Sarah, Pinot noir, and many more. All the other wines improve to a point with bottle aging. Today aging varies from 3 to 18 months in wood and 3-36 months in the bottle. Today, a commercial bottle of wine more than 4 to 5 years old is uncommon and if available, expensive.

The length of aging depends on the desired effect of the individual wine maker. Aging should be done in a dry cool, preferably dark place. The wine should not be exposed to direct sunlight. If you are aging in the bottle, lay the bottle on its side. This keeps the cork moist, which helps it to maintain its swollen size and, therefore, form an affective seal against oxidation. Bottles with screw caps for seals should not be stored for long periods of time. They are very susceptible to oxidation since the seal is not affective against air.

Why age at all? It is believed that a very slow diffusion of oxygen is carried out through the wood, slow enough to avoid damage due to oxidation. This limited oxidation produces desirable changes. The limited oxidation contributes flavor and extracts, causing the wine to become more complex while mellowing many of the harsh flavors. Depending on the relative humidity, the water, and alcohol content slowly evaporates, causing an air space to form in the barrels. This air space is known as 'head space'. Managing the head space is an important part of the aging process. The addition of wine to fill up the barrel is known as topping, Constant topping off of the barrels is of extreme importance. The longer the wine is exposed to air, the greater the damage because of oxidation. Barrels must be regularly topped off every 2 to 4 weeks. It is necessary; therefore, it is necessary to have many different sized vessels to keep them full since the amount of wine is constantly changing. By law, one may use a different type of wine for topping off barrels. In some modern wineries, where wine is stored in bulk, wine is maintained with a layer of inert gas such as nitrogen or carbon dioxide to prevent oxidation.

Wood aging of red wines is recommended for experienced winemakers. One must know how to properly prepare a barrel and maintain them. They take extra space, skill, and work. Oak barrels also add great expensive to your wine making.

10. Clarification:

Clarification is the process by which all the fine particles, called colloids, suspended in the wine are removed. These colloids induce turbidity (cloudiness) in the wine. The clearer the wine, the cleaner the taste, and the more aesthetic pleasure one can get from their efforts.

It is rare for a wine to become brilliantly clear by natural settling. Fining agents are added in small amounts which absorb or combine chemically and/or physically with the colloids to neutralize their electric charges, causing them to agglomerate and gravitate to the bottom of the vessel with time. The home winemaker has a choice of several fining agents from which to choose:

1) Bentonite, which is diatomaceous earth,

2) Egg white

3) Gelatin

4) Activated charcoal

5) Casein and a number of commercially protein-based fining agents.

The common most used fining agent is Bentonite. It is effective at removing proteins or peptide materials. Activated charcoal, gelatin, casein, and others may be also used and assist in removing unstable tannins and other pigments.

The amount of fining agent added is between 0.01-0.015% w/v. Tests on small portions of wine should be made to determine the optimum dosage for each individual wine. The protein binds the colloids, forming a coagulum, which slowly settles to the bottom, over a period of several days to a few weeks. This leaves the wine clear with sediment of coagulum on the bottom of the vessel. This is removed by racking off the clear wine.

A major factor in this reaction is the amount of tannins in the wine. Insufficient tannin or an excess of clarifying agent can retard clarification of the wine. Red wines which, by nature, are high in tannin generally clarify well and this process removes of some of the astringency caused by the tannin may be desirable since it mimics to some extent the aging process. White wines may need tannin added to them to achieve an efficient, satisfactory clarification. Note that most clarifying agents reduce the intensity of the color of red wines and lighten the color of white wines.

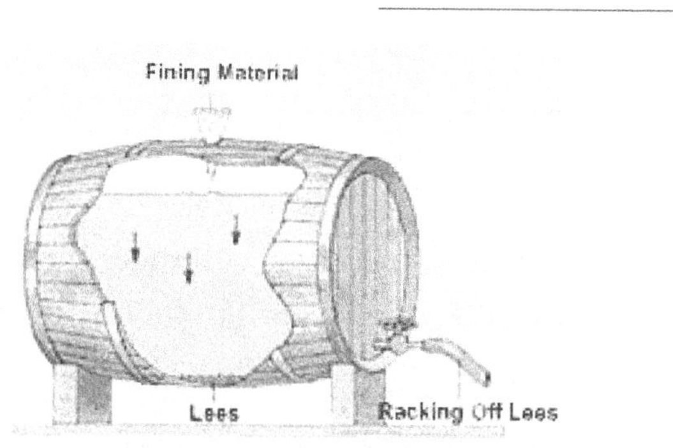

FIGURE 11. HOW FINING Agents Work

11. Blending

The most secret formula of any winery is how, what, and to what percentage that they blend wines. Commercially wines are blended for several reasons:

1. Increase production of varietal wines by adding legal amounts of lesser quality wines.
2. To increase the complexity of the wine.
3. To alter the alcohol content, which is very important in cherry production.
4. Maintain a uniform product.

THERE IS OFTEN VARIATION in flavor, color and alcohol content of various lots of wine of the same type made in the same year. To produce a uniform product in which each bottle will be as good (we hope) as the previous one, it is desirable to blend the various lots together. The flavor of wine is controlled in part by the amount of tannin, total acid, sugar, alcohol and volatile acids. Not all of these are possible for the home winemaker to analyze with his limited resources. What can be detected visually and by taste without difficulty is the amount of sugar, alcohol, total acid and the color.

There is a simple algebraic formula for blending:

$A = \underline{m\text{-}b}$

$B = a\text{-}m$

A = the weight of one component of the mixture and its concentration in percent = 'a,'

B = the Weight of the second component of the mixture and its concentration in percent = 'b.'

m = the desired percent of the factor to be blended.

Example:

Suppose one has two lots of wine. The first lot is at 14% alcohol and the second lot is at 11% alcohol. You desire a wine with 13% alcohol.

In this situation a = 14, b = 11, m = 13.

Then <u>A = m-b = 13-11=2</u>

B = a-m = 14-13=1

or one needs twice the amount of lot A than of lot B to reach the desired alcohol level of 13%.

Pearson Square Method:

Another easy method is a geometric representation that can be used for computing the ratio of two ingredients of a mixture, Step 1. First draw a simple rectangle:

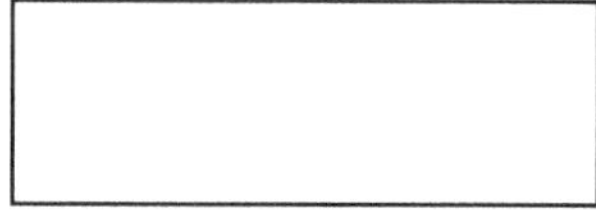

STEP 2. IN THE UPPER left-hand corner place, the concentration of one ingredient. In the lower left had corner place the concentration of the second ingredient. In the center write the desired concentration and subtract in the direction of the right side diagonally.

Example: One lot of wine contains 11.5% alcohol, the second 14% alcohol. The desired concentration is 12.5% alcohol.

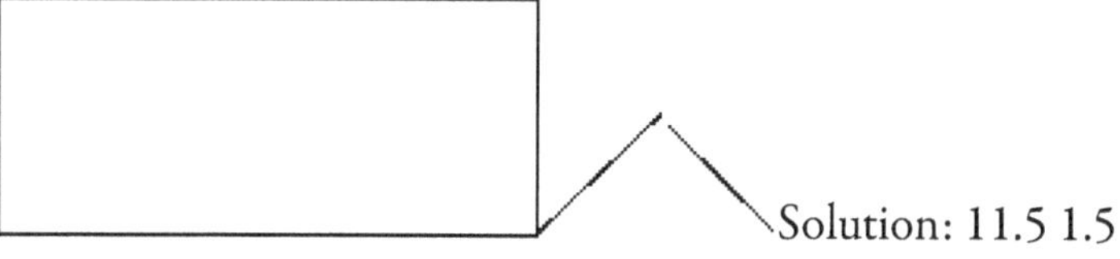

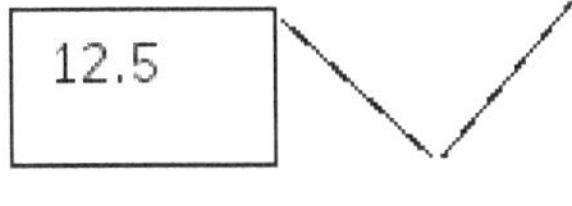

14.0 1.0

The home winemaker may not always have exact figures available. Therefore, estimations by trial and error are necessary. This is still desirable since one would like to enjoy his hard-earned wine bottle after bottle with the same degree of pleasure.

Color is often a problem in wine making. It is often advisable to blend in at the crush a variety with red-colored juice, such as Rubired or Royalty. Alternatively, a small lot of wine of one of these varieties can be made to enhance the quality of the color. These two varieties are both good for blending since they impart little flavor of their own.

Blending is also done between different ages of Sherries. This is known as solera sherry. It is done to produce a uniform product year after year.

Below is a table of typical wine varieties, their tastes and aromas. The home wine maker can use this cart as a guide to blending his wines to make them more complex or reach flavors and aromas that he/she enjoys.

Table of Wine Flavors and Aromas

Variety	Flavors	Aroma
White Wines		
Riesling	Fresh Apples	
Gewürztraminer	Spicy, Rose Petal, Peach, ,Lychee	Honey Sweet Cabbage
Chardonnay	Rich Citrus (Lemon, (Grapefruit New Oak Barrels Adds A Buttery Tone	Mineral Or Mint
Sauvignon Blanc	Suggesting Bell Pepper Or Freshly Mown ,Grass, Apple	Smokey Qualities
Muscat	Peach, Rose Petal, Spicy	Pungent Floral
Pinto Gris	Delicate Citrus And Fruity	Mildly Floral

Viognier	Orange, Fruity, Mint	Buttery, Vanilla
Pinot Blanc	Almond Apple	Buttery, Fruity Hazelnut
Red Wines		
Shiraz	Spicy, Black current	Musk, Earth Truffle
Merlot	Black-Cherry Herbal, Currant	Coconut, Oaky, Smoke
Pinot Noir	Cranberry, Cherry, Raspberry	Fruity, Cherry, Plum Strawberry
Zinfandel	Nectarine, Raspberry, Sour Cherry	Tutti-Fruiti, Candy
Alicante Bouschet	Tienturier Adds	

Deep   Red
      Color

12. Bottling

The final episode in our drama of wine making is bottling the product. Before bottling wine, one should test a sample because it is the last opportunity for any manipulations to improve the quality of the wine.

Checklist:

1) Is the wine the color you desire? If not, what can be done?

a) Too much color. This can be reduced by the use of a clarifying agent such as activated charcoal.

b) Weak color. This can be improved by blending with a deeper colored wine.

2) Clarity. Take a large clean wine glass and fill it ½ to 3/4 full of wine. Grasp the glass by the stem and raise it up toward a good source of light and examine it for any turbidity. If there is a problem, add a fining agent and then rack the wine.

3) Acid content. Taste the wine. This is done by slowly sipping a small amount of wine into your mouth over your tongue at the same time sucking in large quantities of air. Swirl the wine around your mouth for about 3 to 6 seconds and then spit it out and wash your mouth with water.

a) If the wine is flat, add tartaric acid or blend with a high acid wine,

b) If the wine is too acidic for your taste add a carefully calculated amount of calcium carbonate.

Once you have finished with all the final manipulations, your wine is ready to be bottled. For a longer shelf life, the preferred method of bottling wine is to use cork plugs. Screw caps are easier, but allow too much air in which causes the oxidation of the wine.

How to insert a cork in a bottle? The corks should be soaked in water with 75 ppm SO_2 until the corks soften and become pliable. There are many corking devices for the home winemaker. All the devices work on the same general principle. The wet cork must be squeezed through a hole which is directly connected to the mouth of the bottle, but somewhat smaller in diameter. This is done by squeezing the cork through a V-shaped funnel, which causes the cork to be compressed. Corks must be wetted before use. Once the cork is in the mouth of the bottle, it expands, completely filling the space. The cork will maintain this excellent seal if it is kept wet. If the cork dries out, then air will penetrate the wine and cause oxidation. This is the reason all corked wine bottles should be kept lying down to allow constant contact between the wine and the cork.

Figure 12. Various Corking Devices for the Home Winemaker

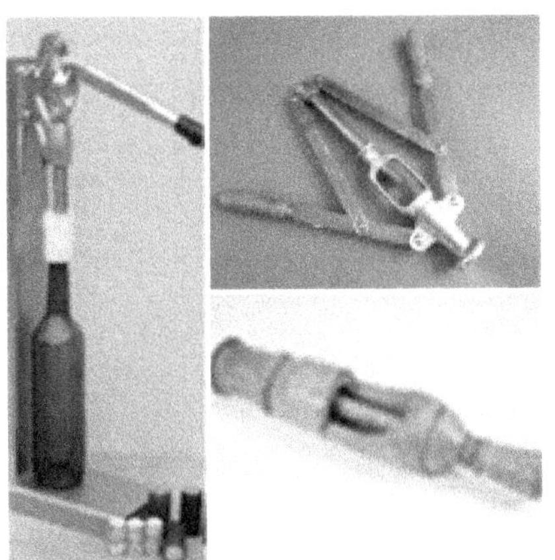

VII. THE EEFECT OF TEMPERATURE ON WINE PRODUCTION

Effect of Temperature on Wine Production

The control of temperature throughout the winemaking process is crucial for the production of fine wines. Temperature plays a significant part from the ripening of the fruit and continues until it reaches the customer. The best quality grapes of the best varieties may not result in superior wines if the proper temperature control is not maintained throughout the entire wine-making process.

Temperature control is important because:

a) High temperatures during fermentation (30 to 36°C) are detrimental to yeast and decrease their growth rate. Reduced growth slowed down the rate of fermentation and at temperatures above 37°C fermentation stops.

b) High fermentation temperatures increase the chances of Lactobacillus sp. contamination and increases the development of detrimental and toxic products of the yeast.

c) At high temperatures more alcohol is evaporated during fermentation, thus reducing the yield of alcohol/amount sugar.

d) High fermentation temperatures decrease the aromas and flavors of white wines,

e) Excessive temperatures during storage induce a general instability in the wine.

f) If the temperature is too hot (>30°C) or too cold (<15°C) during the initial stage of the fermentation of red wines, then color and flavor extraction will decrease.

g) Low (<10 °C) aging temperatures slow the aging process to a point where it is uneconomical.

Below is a table which outlines the recommended temperature ranges for a number of wine-making processes.

Recommended Temperatures for Some Wine-making Processes

Temperature values are given in °C.

Wine -

Type Stabilization <u>Crush</u> <u>Fermentation</u> <u>Cellar Market</u>

White:

Dry 13-18 10-16 7-16 10-18 13-24

Sweet 13-18 10-16 8-18 10-18 13-24

Red

Dry 13-24 18-29 20-30 10-18 13-24

Sweet 18-24 18-29 20-30 13-18 13-24

DESSERT:

Red 21-32 21-30 20 to 30 15-21 13-24

White 21-32 20-26 7 to 16 15-21 13-24

Sherry 21-32 21-29 23 to 25 15-21 13-24

Sparkling*—— 10-15.5^ 6 to 12 13-18 13-24

* Made form a blend of dry table wines

^ For the secondary fermentation, whether, bottle or bulk.

Effect of Temperature on the Fruit

The chemical composition of grapes is greatly affected by the ambient air temperature during ripening. To produce good wines, the fruit must be closely supervised before harvesting. In warm growing climates like Israel, there is a rapid change in the amount of organic acids and sugars during fruit maturation. Hot weather at the end of the season causes a rapid drop in total acid and an equally rapid increase in the sugar content. Alcohol yield is also affected by the accumulated heat at the time of picking. Warmer years produce more alcohol per degree of must sugar.

The actual time of harvesting is also important. Grapes in hot countries like Israel that are exposed to direct sunlight can reach temperatures above 60°C. To reduce this excess latent heat to proper fermenting temperatures would be far too expensive. Grapes should be harvested first thing in the morning as to limit the amount of temperature modification the must will require to reach proper fermenting temperatures.

The Effect of Temperature on Wine Quality.

The quality of white table wines is increased when the must is fermented to 10 to 16°C. With red wines, there is an optimum temperature for color and flavor extraction from the skins between 18 to 30°C. Low temperatures do not extract sufficient color and higher temperatures extract more color, but much of it is unstable. Temperatures above 50°C tend to produce undesirable aromas which have been described as horsey or barn-like. The total acidity is also affected by temperature. The maximum total titratable acid is achieved when the must is fermented between 2 to 27ºC. Some other effects of temperature on the chemical composition of wine are:

1) Fermentation of red wines at high temperatures encourage malo-lactic fermentation during the regular fermentation, thus lowering the total acid content.

2) The loss of aromas and alcohols increases with the increase in temperature and.

3) Prolonged fermentation at low temperatures with high sugar increases the volatile acid content.

The quality of white wines, made from moldy grapes improve, if fermented at somewhat higher temperatures than normal. It is traditional to age sweet wines at warmer temperatures than table wines. Controlled heat treatments can produce flavors in dessert wines. Baked sherry requires prolonged heat (49 to 6O°C) treatment (six weeks to months) depending on the "baked character desired. Superior flavor is achieved by baking at lower temperatures.

Temperature control during the secondary fermentation that produces sparkling wines is also important. The yeast starter used for the fermentation should be acclimated to the temperature and alcohol level prior to use. The best quality sparkling wines are fermented below 15.5°C. At low temperatures, the wines have a fruity aroma and cleaner taste. After the completion of fermentation, the bottles of sparkling wines should be stored at 13 to 15.5°C to allow controlled yeast autolysis. At warmer temperatures, undesirable flavors develop from the rapid degradation of the yeast. When served cold, sparkling wines maintain their level of CO_2 much longer.

VIII. WINE MAKING

Table wines were traditionally intended to be consumed at meals. As one learns more about wine, you find tradition plays an important role in the world of wine.

Dry White Table Wines:

W ith an understanding of the operations involved in winemaking, one can begin to deal with making specific wines. Only home winemakers who are experienced and have all the proper equipment and conditions should attempt to make quality white wines at home. White wines are delicate. The two most difficult problems the home winemaker faces with white wines are:

1) The fermentation of these wines must be between 10 to 16°C and

2) They are exceedingly susceptible to oxidation.

White table wines are preferred light in color, ranging from pale yellow to gold, fruity, tart with a distinctive varietal flavor. This may be achieved by the use good grapes of varieties that have distinct flavors (see the table in the section on Grapes).

Step 1. Pick 5 to 15% of the total amount of grapes that will be used 3 weeks early at around 15° Brix. The must will be high in acid, and this can be a source of natural tartaric acid for blending later. Treat this lot of wine exactly as the main fermentation. This step is recommended for all the wine you will make unless you have a source of commercial tartaric acid.

Step 2. Prepare a pure wine yeast starter. It should be of 3 to 5% of the total amount of grapes of your main fermentation. Use the same variety of grapes, or one that has a neutral taste so it would not interfere with the distinct flavor you are trying to achieve. It is important to begin the starter, neither too soon nor too late. It should be actively fermenting when it is added to the main lot of must. Starter can be increased about 1:10 every week.

Step 3. On the day you plan to begin your main fermentation, start all your procedures as early as possible in the morning. This will help keep the grapes and must at a low temperature. The grapes should be carefully examined and sort out as many diseased berries as possible. The grapes are then transferred from the picking bins to the vessel used for crushing (by hand, foot or machine). Crush a random sample of berries and make your first analysis for acid, sugar, and pH. White wines should have at least 0.8% total acid as tartaric and the must should range from 20 to 23° Brix. The grapes are then crushed, destemmed, SO2 added and immediately pressed. The clearer the must, the fruitier the taste is, but with a simple, uncomplicated flavor. Cloudy musts produce wines with a more complex character.

A comparison made between wines of clear vs. cloudy musts showed that the clear musts produced more superior wines. Whether to ferment with a cloudy or clear must will depend on the type of character one wants in their wine. The complex hearty flavor is due to fusel oils alcohols with more than 2 carbons, which form as a result of contact of air with the suspended colloids in the must. To achieve this flavor and body, the must be left in contact with the skins longer.

Chardonnay is the recommended variety. The maximum must-skin contact should not extend over 16 hours. The problem in this process is excessive exposure to air, which will cause damage due to oxidation.

This can be solved by the use of blanketing the must with an inert gas (like nitrogen or carbon dioxide). This requires a source of gas, and air-tight containers, to prevent leakage.

Step 4. Fermentation: Most white wines are fermented at 10 to 15°C. It takes between 12 to 18 days to complete the active phase of fermentation. When sugar is converted into ethanol, heat is given off. To control this increase in temperature and maintain the proper low temperatures for the white must to ferment, it is necessary to refrigerate. The lower the temperature, the slower the fermentation.

At 1 to 3°C, the fermentation can take as long as six months to finish. These long fermentations produce unique flavors and aromas, an important criterion of a superior wine. At home, this is difficult to achieve. The simplest way to control the temperature of the fermentation is to place the fermenting vessels in an air-conditioned room. Small lots (one to five liters) can be fermented in your refrigerator at 4°C. Fill the bottle 1/2-3/4 full and place an air lock on it.

Let the wine ferment during the day in the refrigerator and at night when the temperature is below 15°C allow the wine to ferment outside.

This will speed up the fermentation, so it should not take longer than six to nine weeks.

Step 5. Fermentation is concluded when no more bubbles are observed in the airlock for over a 1/2 hour. Now test the wine for total acid and pH. If the pH is low i.e., less than 3.5, add 70-90 ppm SO_2. If the pH is higher, add acid if available and then add 90 to 120 ppm SO_2.

Step 6 Allow the wine to settle for seven to ten days and then rack the wine off the lees. You find that the upper 1/3 is clear, the middle 1/3 is slightly cloudy and the bottom third next to the lees is the least clear.

If possible, try to keep these fractions separate to facilitate later rackings. Remember, after racking to keep all the vessels with wine filled to the brim and sealed to prevent oxidation.

Step 7. Clarify the wine with bentonite as it removes polymeric phenols and heat labile proteins. Then rack the wine of the bentonite complex after 15 to 25 days.

Step 8. Analyze the wine and make all corrections and adjustments.

Step 9. Make a final racking, if necessary, and blend if desired.

Step 10 Bottle. If you have kept lots separately during the fermentation, make certain to label them properly so you can compare the effects of your procedures on the final product.

White wines are best stored in a cool, dark environment. They are particularly sensitive to heat and sunlight.

Dry Red Table Wines

Step 1. Prepare starter.

Step 2. Pick grapes at 22 to 24° Brix. Cull for all diseased berries.

Step 3. Crush and destem the grapes.

Step 4. Add SO2 at 8 to 120 ppm and wait for two hours.

Step 5. After two hours, add starter. Note: Disregard steps 4 & 5 for natural fermentation. Modify steps 3, 4, and 5 to ferment by *maceration carbonique*. The initial fermentation should take place in an open vessel to facilitate Cap management.

Step 6. Cap Management. Red wines are fermented with the skins for the first week. Red pigment and much of the flavor is found in the skins of the grapes. Most grape juice is clear it is, therefore, possible to make white wines from red varieties. The longer the skins are kept in contact with the must, the more color will be obtained. As the must ferments, the rising amount of alcohol acts as an efficient solvent on the skins, releasing an increasing amount of color. For a rose wine, ferment with the skins for about 3 days. For a full red colored table wine, ferment with the skins for 5 to 8 days depending on the variety.

Fermentation gives off large amounts of heat. The skins in the must float to the top and form an insulating layer called a cap. The cap must be broken up and mixed with the fermenting must for two reasons. First is to reduce the cap's insulating effect, and to allow the built-up heat to escape. Second is to allow better contact between the fermenting must and the skins. This interaction allows for better extraction of color and flavor. The cap should be mixed back into the must 2 to 3 times a day. This can be accomplished without difficulty with a wood or plastic stick. Using any metals other than stainless steel causes heavy metal contamination. The fermentation would be maintained at room temperature, 20 to 28 °C.

Step 7. When the desired amount of color has been extracted from the skins, the skins, seeds, and other debris should be removed. Drain off as much of the must as possible. Then sieve the remaining mixture through gauze. When you have gathered 1 to 3 kg of cap in the gauze, press the mixture by wringing it out. This procedure is messy, so be sure to:

1) Wear old clothes or an apron,

2) Have something to throw the pomace away in and

3(Have plenty of water available for cleaning up.

Step 8. After another 6 to 10 days (depending on the variety and temperature of the fermentation) one will observe a definite slackening off in the rate of the fermentation. At this time, the must should be transferred to a sealed vessel with an airlock.

Step 9. With the completion of fermentation allow the wine to settle for 7 to 10 days and then rack.

Step 10. Analyze the wine for as many characteristics you have facilities for (either chemically or organoleptically). Carry out required adjustments and rack if necessary.

Step 11. Clarify; the wine. If you want to use egg whites, whip them up previous to adding them to the wine. Blend the egg whites in the same manner as one would fold them into a cake batter. Allow clarifying agent to settle for 10 to 18 days depending on how fast the material settles, then rack. Make sure you have sufficient vessels to put the clarified wine into so that all the vessels will be one hundred percent full.

Step 12. Aging: The aging of red wines is fundamentally different from white wines. Aging wines in wood is for red wines (except for Chardonnay). All full colored red wines benefit from some aging in wood. The preferred wood for barrels in most wineries is oak. In various countries, other types of wood are used to a small degree (such as redwood in California). Since small (10 to 30 liters) oak barrels are expensive and difficult to find for most home winemakers, do not age in wine.

Partial substitutes have been experimented with. Oak chips or sawdust have been added to wine. It cannot replace the aging in barrels but adds some oak bouquet and flavor

.

Step 13. After the initial six months of aging, wine should be tested every two-three months to determine whether it has reached the desired effect. This process can take as long as two years. Upon completion check the wine for clarity.

Step 14. The wine is now ready for bottling and labeling and if desired more aging in the bottle. Bottle aging can be from 3 to 36 months. I recommend that you experiment with different amounts of aging in the bottle and observe the differences in bouquet and flavor with time.

Sweet Wines

Home winemakers all over the world have been using almost every variety available (or combinations of them) for making sweet wine. In many wine-producing countries, some varieties have been favored over others mostly because of the varieties ability to reach 26° Brix or more. For example, in France the famous sauternes are made from Semillon and Sauvignon Blanc. In Hungary, Tokay is made from Furmint.

Sweet table wines more often than not have less than 14% alcohol and range from 5 to 10%

Classification of Wine by Sugar Content

Wine type Sugar Content

Dry > 0 . 2%

*Mellow 0.2-0.5

Sweet 0.5-10%

*= At this sugar content the wine is not sweet, but it is softer and distinctly different from dry table wines.

To make sweet wine from grapes without adding sugar, one must allow the grapes to reach at least 26° Brix. Some home winemakers allow the grapes to partially raising on the vine before picking them. This, however, adds the caramel odor and flavor to the wine, which is often undesirable.

By far, most sweet wines made at home are made with the addition of sugar. The amount of sugar depends on individual tastes. It ranges from 1 kg sugar: 10 kg grapes to 1 kg sugar: 2 kg grapes. The majority of home winemakers add the sugar right after crushing. Most of these people are not concern about the precise amount of residual Sugar there will be. However, if you want a precise amount of sweetness, a hydrometer or refractometer is needed. A hydrometer measures cylinder buoyancy depends on the amount of sugar in a fluid. It is a graduated glass with a weighted tail. It is placed into the must and its amount of sugar in the must. The sweet wines are easy to make or protect it against microbial contamination at one's the home.

It is difficult for the home winemaker to achieve slightly sweet wines with 0.5 to 2.0% sugar. These wines are very susceptible to secondary fermentation and need sterile filtering or pasteurization to keep them for any length of time. Remember, every degree of Brix is converted into approximately 0.55% alcohol.

The abundant variations on procedures of how to make sweet wines are as many as there are winemakers. Below will be outline two variations on making technically sound sweet wines, by natural fermentation and controlled fermentation.

Natural fermentation:

Step 1. Crush and destem.

Step 2a. If you are using grapes with high sugar content, don't plan to add any sugar, allow the must to begin to ferment. This is not recommended for white wines.

Step 2b. If you plan to add sugar in a precise manner, use a hydrometer or refractometer to determine the exact amount of sugar to be added.

Step 3. Allow an additional 2 to 4 days of skin Contact for good color extraction since a slowly fermenting must extracts little color. Then press and continue the fermentation.

Controlled fermentation

Step 1. Crush and destem.

.

Step 2. Add 80 to 120 ppm SO$_2$.

Step 3. If you don't plan to add any additional sugar, go to step 4. However, if you want a sweeter wine follow the procedure in step 2b of natural fermentation.

Step 4. After waiting 2 to 3 hours add active pure wine yeast starter.

All the following steps are identical for both systems.

Step 5. Ferment both red and whites at low temperatures.

Step 6. Rack the wine during fermentation to reduce the yeast population.

Step 7. Add 1 to 2% alcohol during the fermentation. Since wine yeast stop fermenting at 14% alcohol, you will achieve this faster and leave more residual sugar.

Step 8. Termination of the fermentation: If large amounts of sugar are not added to the must to ensure that there will be residual sugar at the completion of fermentation, then the fermentation must be stopped artificially. This can be done by lowering the fermentation temperature, adding large amounts of SO$_2$ (130 to 150 ppm) and then racking the wine soon after, to reduce the yeast population.

Step 9. Allow the wine to settle and then rack. Repeat this once or twice more.

Step 10. Clarify and rack.

Step 11. Stabilization: The best method to maintain low levels of sugar in sweet wines is by sterile filtration and aseptic bottling. These processes are often beyond the capacity of your normal home winemaking operation. The next best procedure to prevent secondary fermentation is adding sorbic acid. It should be added at a rate of

0.5 to 0.08%. It should not exceed more than this because at high concentrations it causes undesirable odors.

Dessert and Appetizer Wines

⸺

Appetizer and Dessert are wines whose alcohol content range between 18-21%. Dessert wines have perceptible amounts of sugar, while appetizer wines are dry or just slightly sweet. The higher levels of alcohol are achieved by adding brandy spirits before completing the fermentation. The addition of alcohol depends on the degree of Brix of the fermenting must. The fermentation can be stopped at what/ever percent of sugar is desired in the final product.

How much Brandy spirits to add?

The formula for determining the amount of brandy spirits to add is:

(A x a) + (B x b) = (A+B) x m.

Where A = weight of wine.

a = % alcohol of the wine.

B = weight of brandy.

b =% alcohol of brandy.

m =% alcohol of desired blend.

Example: You desire the final product to have 20% alcohol and you have brandy at 50% alcohol. The weight of the wine is 40 kg and its alcohol content is 13%, then the amount of brandy needed to fortify the wine to 20% is:

(40 x 13) + (50 x E) = (40 + B) X 20

520 + 5OB =800 + 2OB

3OB = 280

B=9.3 kg of brandy.

BELOW IS A TABLE SHOWING some of the characteristics of some white dessert wines.

White Dessert Wines

<u>Type Flavor Color °Brix</u>

Muscatel distinct Muscat light gold 5-8° Angelica fruity yellow-golden 8-9

White Port light & fruity very light color 6-7

Sweet Sherry

a) Baked raisin or baked pale amber 0-2

b) Aged caramel dark amber 4-6

Because of the great differences in making some of these wines, the duration of some of the processes and that some are rarely made at home, just simple dessert wine making will be discussed. For further details see The Technology of Wine Making, M.A. Amerine et al. (1972).

Production Methods of White Dessert Wines:

Step 1, Harvest the grapes at maximum ° Brix, but without raisins or shriveling, because raisined berries give another taste that is not typical to these types of wine.

Step 2. Crush, destem and add SO_2 (100ppm).

Step 3. Drain and Press. This step is critical because the must is exposed to large quantities of air. This step should be done as quickly as possible.

Step 4. Add pure wine yeast starter and ferment at 10 to 14 °C.

Step 5. Fortification of fermenting musts with brandy spirits. The must is fortified early in the fermentation to ensure that sufficient sugar remains. Below is a list of the necessary sugar content of the must to produce the desired wine.

a) Angelica 18° Brix

b) Muscatel or White Port 16° Brix

c) Sweet Sherry 12° Brix

When wine spirits are added at 15° Brix to make 20% alcohol by volume, the new sugar content of the blend will be approximately 7° Brix. The high alcohol content protects the high sugar content against secondary fermentation.

Step 6. Adding alcohol stops the fermentation. The fortified wine is then allowed to settle for 2 to 4 days and then ranked to remove most of the yeast.

Step 7. Most dessert wines are clarified with bentonite at a rate of 60 gm/100 liters. Allow the wine to settle and rack,

Step 8. Test the resulting wine and make any corrections necessary and rack again if the wine is turbid.

Step 9. Bottle. These wines can be kept for several years because of their high alcohol content. For red dessert wines, the procedure is the same except allow the must to ferment on the skins for 6 to 5 days. Then press the mixture to remove the skins, seeds, and stems. The fermentation of dessert wine should be carried out at 20 to 25°C.

Sparkling Wines

S parkling wines are wines with excess carbon dioxide caused by a secondary fermentation or adding carbon dioxide gas. Producing sparkling wines is outside the scoop of most home winemakers. Only skilled and experienced winemakers should attempt this. It requires one to invest time, money and equipment. This section will, therefore, not be one of practical procedure, but for providing the reader with general information on producing of sparkling wines. With this information, the reader will be far better equipped to understand and select better quality wine.

The induction of carbon dioxide into wine can be accomplished by three processes:

1) Carbonation: the addition of CO_2 gas under pressure at low temperatures into wine.

2) Bottle fermentation-induced secondary yeast fermentation in special reinforced bottles and

3) Bulk fermentation: Induction of a secondary yeast fermentation in large tanks.

The process of carbonation is exactly the same as carbonating any liquid, such as sodas and carbonated fruit juices. The base wines are standard bulk-produced wines. Carbonated wines are popular among people whom are beginners in wine appreciation. There are several samples of this sold here in Israel. Many of them are lower in alcohol (5-9%) and sweet, which adds to their popularity.

Bottle fermentation is a long, difficult and arduous hand process. First prepare the Cuvee. The Cuvee is the base wine for the secondary fermentation, which is made from a blend of wines. Blending is done to promote a base wine with the following attributes: low alcohol, high acid (0.65-O.753%), light color, and a clean, fruity aroma. The carbon dioxide is produced by adding sugar and pure wine yeast starter into each bottle and capturing the CO_2 produced by the fermentation in the bottle. The desired and acceptable amount of pressure of CO_2 in sparkling wines is four atmospheres. To promote one atmosphere of pressure at 10°C, one needs to add four grams of sugar per liter.

Therefore, to produce the needed four atmospheres one must add 16 gm of sugar/liter. The starter should be actively fermenting and be added at the rate of 2 to 3%. The yeast should be of a variety that is low temperature, high pressure tolerant and a heavy. In that manner whose dead cells readily fall out of suspension to the bottom of the bottle. This mixture of wine, yeast, and sugar is known as the triage.

The secondary fermentation takes 4 to 6 weeks to complete. Once the fermentation is completed, the wine is allowed to age on the yeast sediment at least for one year. The autolysis (disintegration of dead cells) of the yeast provides additional desirable flavors (thought to be from amino acids). This is one of the major differences between battle and bulk fermented sparkling wines.

To remove the yeast from the bottle, one must get the yeast to settle out next to the cork at the mouth of the bottle. To accomplish this, the bottles are maintained in racks upside down. The bottles are riddled regularly, i.e., turned right and left to loosen the yeast and cause them to settle at the mouth of the bottle. When riddling is completed, the bottle is 'jolted' by dropping it lightly back into the rack to encourage the downward movement of the yeast.

The bottles are turned 1/8 of a turn every day. As the bottles age, they are moved to racks with increasingly greater angles to ensure that all the yeast will be next to the mouth of the kettle.

There are three methods for removing yeast from the neck of the bottle, which is known as disgorging:

> 1) The first method is the traditional method of quickly removing the cork with its lees and yeast while losing the minimal amount of wine.

2) This is accomplished by freezing a small `plug' of wine next to the cork, where the yeast is located. The bottle is held at a 45° angle and the cork plus the plug is removed. The bottles are immediately sealed in a temporary manner. Since there is a loss of some wine before final bottling additional wine must be added. This is called dosage. It is also an opportunity to alter the sugar or alcohol content if desired. The wine is then permanently sealed and ready for consumption.

3) The Transfer Method: the second system, the wine plus the yeast are collected from many bottles in a large tank. Here the dosage is added. The wine is then filtered and bottled in the original or new bottles.

Metodo Martinotti Method or Bulk fermentation:

The second is the Metodo Martinotti, created and patented by Italian Federico Martinotti (1860 to 1924) in 1895. As mentioned above, a Cuvee is blended and placed in a large tank. To this, the same proportions of sugar and yeast are added to the wine as in bottled fermented sparkling wines. The fermentation is carried at 10 to 14°C for 2 to 4 weeks. Occasionally stir the fermenting wine to avoid thick yeast deposits. Sparkling wine is then racked off and filtered into a finishing tank. The wine is then stabilized for excess tartrates. Cool the wine and the tartrates fall out of the solution. The wine is then transferred into the bottling tank. Here the dosage is added. The final steps are to sterile filter the sparkling wine and bottle it.

Sparkling wine should be kept as cold as possible when being transferred or bottled. It is advisable to maintain the wine under a blanket of nitrogen gas to prevent oxidation and maintain the pressure of the carbon dioxide.

IX. FRUIT WINES

Making fruit wine is popular among home winemakers. Fruit wines are not referred to by varietal names like grapes, but identified by the fruit used to make the wine.

Numerous fruits and non-fruits are made into wine. This includes every fruit you can think of from strawberry, blueberry, kiwi, mango, etc. Wines are made from vegetables, tomato, rhubarb, watermelon, and even onions! Flowers are used to make wine, such as dandelion, carnation, honeysuckle, rose hip, and so on.

The big differences between grape juice and other fruit juices are that grape juice has all the growth nutrients, vitamins and energy sources required to sustain good yeast growth and, therefore, good fermentation of the sugar to alcohol.

In most cases, the percent of alcohol of fruit wines are 5% unless nutrients and or sugar are added to encourage yeast growth. In this section, the fruit wine from available fruit is described in easy step-by-step procedures.

Apple Wine (Cider)

The preferable varieties for making apple cider should be varieties that have a good sugar: acid balance so to provide a good taste to the final product.

Step 1. Pick apples and store them for a few days to develop aroma.

Step 2. Wash and sort out all damaged and diseased apples.

Step 3. Crush and press the apples. Make sure you remove the seeds as they give a bitter taste.

Step 4. Keeving: Cool the juice to 4-8°C and allow the juice to settle. The underlying principle is to remove nutrients from the juice by allowing the pectin to bind to them. This is done at the beginning of the process to ensure a long, slow fermentation. This allows the fermentation to reach a point where there is still residual sugar. Most apple ciders are not fermented to the end and are preferred to be to some extent of sweetness. Keeving allows the cider to be bottled while still sweet and with no fear of excessive re-fermentation later.

Step 5. Sulfur Treatment: Add 50 to 100 ppm SO_2/liter.

Step 6. Check acidity. If below 0.6 gm/L, then add lactic acid to increase the acidity.

Step 7. Fermentation: Fermentation can be carried out naturally, but better results are achieved by the addition of a pure wine yeast starter. Fermentation should be conducted cold (4 to 8°C). This can be done in small amounts in your refrigerator. Fermentation lasts 4 to 6 weeks. After initial fermentation, a secondary fermentation often occurs lasting between 4 to 6 weeks. Often, apple wine undergoes a malo-lactic fermentation.

Step 8. When fermentation finishes, allow the wine to settle and then rack. Repeat this 2 to 3 times.

Step 9. Bottle.

The resulting wines are 5 to 6% alcohol. Dessert wines can be made by blending in neutral high alcohol spirits (see section on dessert wines).

Cherry Wine

Sour cherries are preferable to sweet cherries for making wine, as the acidity of sweet cherries is too low. A blend of sweet and sour cherries can also be used. Crushed cherry pits add some additional flavor to the wine, but do not crush more than 8 to 10% of the pits, because at high concentrations it causes an undesirable flavor.

Step 1. Wash and sort out all damaged and spoiled cherries.

Step 2. Crush. Some people like to leave some cherries whole during the fermentation.

Step 3. Add 75-100 ppm SO2.

Step 4. Wait 2 hours and add 2 to 5% actively fermenting pure wine yeast starter.

Step 5. Ferment in open containers at 15 to 20°C (cool room temperature) for 8 to 10 days and then press.

Step 6. Once the cherry must is fermenting less rapidly, transfer to a closed container with an airlock.

7. After completion of fermentation allow the wine to settle and then rack.

8. If necessary, clarify with bentonite and then rack.

9. Bottle.

10. Enjoy a glass

Plum Wine

Step 1. Crush the plums and add 2 liters of water for every kilogram of fruit.

Step 2. Add 80 to 110 ppm SO_2/L.

Step 3 Wait 2 to 3 hours and add 3 to 5% actively fermenting pure wine yeast starter.

Step 4 Ferment at 20 to 25°C for 8 to 10 days and then press. Additional sugar can be added if desired. The amount will depend on whether a table or dessert wine is desired. The wine should be now in a closed container with an airlock.

Step 5. After fermentation has finished allow the wine to settle and rack. Rack again after it has settled for an additional two weeks.

Step 6 Analyze the wine for sugar and acid content. If the plum wine is low in acid, lactic or citric acid can be added to correct the total acid content. Plum table wine should not be below 0.6% total acid and dessert wine, not below 0.5% total acid.

Step 7 Clarify with bentonite and then rack.

Step 8. If dessert wine is desired fortify now with neutral high alcohol spirits to 20% alcohol. Remember, adding more liquid will lower the acid and sugar content per liter of wine. Therefore, take this into consideration when doing step 6.

Step 9. Bottle.

Pomegranate Wine.

Step 1. Do not crush, but press the whole fruit.

Step 2. Add sugar to reach 21 to 23° Brix.

Step 3. Add 70 to 100 ppm SO2 and wait 2 to 3 hours.

Step 4. Add 2 to 3% actively fermenting pure wine yeast starter.

Step 5. Ferment at 20 to 25°C for 8 to 12 days. When the fermentation has slowed down, transfer to vessel with an airlock.

Step 6. Upon the completion of fermentation allow the wine to settle and then rack, Repeat this procedure after 15 to 20 days.

Step 7. Fortify to 20% alcohol if a dessert wine is desired and adjust its sugar and acid content.

Step 8. Bottle.

Honey Wine (Mead).

Mead contains a comparatively high alcohol content compare to beer and table wines. There are three essential ingredients to making mead: honey, yeast, and water. Since honey is the fundamental component, the resulting mead should have a very nice bouquet to it.

Mead is classified by the flavoring added to it. They are:

- *Traditional*: mead made with honey, water, and yeast.
- *Metheglin*: mead made with added herbs or spices, such as cloves or cinnamon.
- Melomel: mead made with adding fruit or fruit juice to traditional mead.
- Cyser: mead made with apples or apple juice.
- Pyment: mead made with grapes or grape juice.
- Hippocras: is a spiced pyment.
- Sack: a stronger (more alcohol content) mead, made with a higher honey to water ratio.

There are many flavored honeys available, be sure to select one with a mild flavor. Honey from onion flowers will make a wine difficult to some palates.

Step 1. Dilute the honey with good quality water at a rate of 1.5 kg honey to 4 liters of water in a large pot and then pour it into your primary fermenting vessel.

Step 2. Add K-meta-bisulfate at a rate of 80 to 100 ppm SO2. This will kill the wild yeast. The wild yeast cannot ferment your honey to a high percentage of alcohol. Mix the solution well and let it sit for 24 hours.

Step 3. Check sugar concentration. Most people like to start around 22° Brix. Higher concentrations will produce a Sack mead.

Step 4. Hydrating Yeast: This should be done 15 minutes before the end of step 2. Warm 50 ml of water to 40°C and add the dry wine yeast. Mix thoroughly to break up any clumps and let it sit 15 minutes. Since this mixture has no nutrients for the yeast to grow, don't leave it beyond the required time, the yeast will begin to die.

Step 5. Unlike grape, juice honey is deficient in the nutrients necessary for good yeast growth. Add yeast food, like $(NH4)2O4$, because honey is lacking in many of the elements needed for good growth. For each liter of diluted honey acid, 14 gm $(NH4)2HPO4$, 1 gm potassium bitartare and 0.25 gm magnesium chloride or calcium chloride. All of these can be dissolved by heating them in a small amount of diluted honey and then stir into the main solution.

.

Step 6. Yeast. Now add the hydrated yeast.

Step 7. Mead will take a long time to ferment. Fermentation times can be measured in months. Mead likes to ferment a little warmer than beer (23 to 28°C). Rack mead while it is fermenting. If you make any kind of mead beside traditional, you will have to rack about a week after removing the bits of fruit and spices that settle out. Rack periodically after that to get the mead off the dead yeast and other matter that settles out every 3 to 6 weeks depending on the rate of fermentation and settling. This improves the flavor and clarifies the mead.

Initial fermentation of melomels made with fruit (not just juice) is easiest in a food-grade plastic pail so you can strain out the fruit before racking. Except for this, glass carboys with fermentation locks are an excellent fermentation vessels.

Step 8. Conduct an acid sugar ratio evaluation and make adjustments.

Step 9. After the fermentation is complete (when there is less than one bubble per minute), allow the wine to settle out the lees. Clarify end rack again. The wine can be preserved for periods of time, but it needs flash pasteurization.

Step 10. Bottle: Make sure all your equipment and bottles are clean.

X. SENSORY EVALUATION

———

The sensory evaluation of wine is the analysis of wine by our senses of the taste, sight and smell. Wine evaluation is very subjective because our sensory evaluation is greatly influenced by physiological, psychological and cultural factors. Serious wine "tasters' try to eliminate as many of these factors by tasting wines blindly. A blind tasting means that the wine taster receives a sample of the wine with absolutely no previous knowledge of its origin, type, producer or age.

The aesthetic value of wine is one of the most important and difficult factors for the wine taster to evaluate. Different wine gives varying degrees of Pleasure to different individuals. The greater our knowledge of wine, the more competent we are to judge wines and the greater our capacity to enjoy a greater diversity of wines.

One's initial reaction to an aesthetic object such as wine is subjective:

Either we like it or we don't. Our evaluation and pleasure of wine is a learned response based on our knowledge and sensory pleasure of wine. As we taste more wines, learn to identify varietal aromas, and flavor, our appreciation of wine will increase.

There are many misnomers that need to be elucidated concerning wines. Never depend on the reputation of a variety, name of a producer, area or origin or price to judge the quality of a wine. In our modern world of high-pressure marketing, be careful not to be swayed by flashy labels or sexy advertisements. The single accurate test of any wine is a blind tasting. The intelligent wine connoisseur will depend on their accumulated knowledge and sensory perception of a wine, ignore the advertising agencies and wine 'experts'.

A few other misnomers about wine should also be cleared up, which are not true.

1) Wine judges are born into certain families. These are snobs. The skill to judge a wine is a learned skill. Only people with medical problems with their organoleptic facilities cannot judge wines.

2) Not just experts can fully enjoy quality and characteristics of wines. The expert may understand why he enjoys a particular wine, but pleasure derived from a wine is individual and almost only subjective.

3) Well, known producers of wine do not always produce superior wines. There are good years and not so good years. Wines of certain regions don't automatically make them superior to wines of other regions.

4) Not all wines improve with aging. White wines may improve to some extent after a few years; however, additional aging adds nothing. Excessive aging can easily lead to oxidation in white wines. Not all red wines need to be stored in wood. Excessive wood aging leads to an overpowering oaky or woody odor. Upon aging certain varietal wines, they will acquire nuances of bouquet that as young wines they lack. With excessive aging, red wines are also subject to oxidation and browning. To praise a wine because it is old and aged for a long time, ignores its overall characteristics. This is a gross error a knowledgeable wine taster should never make.

5) Decanting of red wines before serving does not always improve its quality. It is effective with wines that have some defect, such as excessive gassiness or an off odor that will evaporate before it is drunk. Decanting is more likely to improve a young wine than an old wine since old wines quality can deteriorate rapidly ones exposed to air.

6) Never depend on the price of a wine as a guide to its quality. Prices are a matter of marketing. Also, if you equate price and quality together, you may find cheaper wines (though not the best) are a far better buy for the money.

9) In this section, the use of each of our individual senses involved in sensory evaluation will be discussed.

Our sense of sight accounts for two aspects of wine evaluation, color, and appearance. Vision is the sense we use first when evaluating a new wine. The color of the wine is the first thing we see. The evaluation of color is subjective and its appreciation is learned with time. Some colors are by nature more pleasing to the eye, such as a clear bright red vs. a brown, or a light yellow over dark amber. Our response to color seems to originate from an acquired knowledge for what color is appropriate for a particular wine type. People will enjoy a brown sherry, but not a brown White Riesling. The color of wine is not static. The color of wine darkens with time. No white wine is truly white. They range from an under ripe greenish tint to amber. The riper the grapes the more pigment is found in the wine. White wine kept in wood casks or in the bottle for a few years will turn amber or even brown.

Rose wines should be pink with no tint of brown, purple or tawny. Most of the time these tints show excessive aging or oxidation of the wine a purple tint shows a high pH (low acid) wine. Low acid wines are the result in most cases by excessive malo-lactic fermentation.

The majority of world wines are red, with a wide range of acceptable colors depending on the variety and age. Only teinturiers (red juiced varieties) will have a natural purple red color. The desired color for most commercial wines is ruby red. Red wines that are bottle aged develop an amber (or tawny) tint.

The tint (hue) and depth of color (lightness) tell us much about the condition of a wine. It can alert us to be on the lookout for desirable or undesirable aromas and flavors. The third parameter of color is its purity. It takes experience and a great deal of learning to judge each of these three aspects of color. The human eye is most sensitive to the yellow-green region of the color spectrum. This makes judging the characteristic of red wines more difficult than white wines. The apparent tint of a wine is also greatly modified by the color of the background and the source of the light.

Therefore, it is crucial to examine wines under a constant and adequate source of light. Fluorescent and mercury arc lamps can produce false tints in a wine. There is no perfect guide, but with experience, one learns to recognize the appropriate color and tint for each type of wines. The lack of color can be due to the use of a high pH wine, oxidation, excess metal content and other wine disorders. High iron content in white wines cause a greenish-yellow tint and in red wines an iridescent film on the surface. With this information, never judge a wine in a dimly lit place such as a restaurant.

Below is a table outlining the different preferred colors of wines?

The Preferred Color of Different Wine Types.

<u>Wine Type preferred Color</u>

Table Wines

White:

White Riesling greenish yellow-yellow

Chablis light yellow

Chardonnay yellow-light gold

Sauvignon Blanc yellow-light gold

Red:

Pinot noir low-medium red

Petite Sarah low-medium red

Cabernet Sauvignon medium red

Ruby Cabernet medium red

Rose:

All Roses clear pink

Sweet:

Reds medium-deep red

Hock yellow-light gold

Sauternes yellow-gold

Sherry

Dry baked light amber

Sweet baked medium amber

Fino light amber

Dessert

White: Muscatel light amber-gold

Port very light

Red:

Tawny Port amber-red

Ruby Port ruby red

Champagne

Red red

Rose pink

White light yellow

The appearance of a wine is judged on its clarity or freedom from suspended material.

1) Poor winemaking practice,

2) Aging has left a deposit of dead yeast cells or

3) Microbial spoilage. Cloudiness is always a negative characteristic and a sign that one of the above-mentioned problems exist.

Odor

T hough color can be beautiful, it is an external affair. The most important factor in the quality of a wine is its odor. It is more important than taste because of the almost unlimited variety of subtle differences that are possible. Our olfactory nerve in our nose is responsible for our ability to sense different odors. Our sense of smell is extremely sensitive to even trace amounts of aromatic substances. The olfactory nerve is a small region in the upper part of the nose. In the normal course of breathing, little air passes this region. To more accurately detect various aromatic compounds, air must be diverted to the olfactory region. This is done by sniffing. A good wine judge will learn to sniff well. People subject to colds or allergies are handicapped in this region. The most effective way of utilizing our olfactory nerve for wine evaluation is to place the nose into the glass above the wine and give a quick forceful sniff. Wait 15 to 50 seconds before repeating it as not to fatigue the olfactory nerve.

Not all odors come to the olfactory region by breathing. Wine taken into the mouth warms up quickly, causing the evaporation of more aromatic compounds which then move internally from the mouth to the olfactory region. These internally sensed odors are an important part of the factors that make up what we call flavor.

Recent research has shown that the most important aromatic compounds in wine are derived from chemicals called monoterpenes. These are found in two forms; bound and unbound. Unbound monoterpenes are very aromatic. A new natural enzyme has been found that releases the bound forms to unbound, increasing the natural aroma of the wine.

The desirable and pleasant odors of wine arise from four main sources. They are:

1. The variety of the grape,

2. Byproducts of fermentation,

3. Treatments given to the wine during processing and

4. The aging process.

Odors originating from the grape itself are called aromas. The odors originating from the fermentation, processing or aging are called bouquet. The table below lists different varieties and their characteristic aromas.

WINE VARIETIES AND their Characteristic Aromas

White wines

Muscats

Muscat of Alexander: Floral with overtones of apricot and mint.

Muscat of Hamburg: They have a pronounced odor of Flora linalool. Once this floral odor is recognized, it is easy to identify.

French Colombard: Mildly distinctive aroma. Overripe grapes give a too powerful odor.

White Riesling: Fruity-apple-like.

Chardonnay: Fig-apple-melon-like odor. Its odor is changed by wood or bottle aging from simple and fruity to very complex.

Sauvignon Blanc: Distinctively spicy or weedy (herbaceous). It improves when grow in cool regions.

Semillon: Though very different from Chardonnay,

it is also described as fig-apple-melon.

Less and Non-Distinctive odors:

Burger, Syltanina, Chenin Blanc and Sylvaner

Red Wines:

Cabernet Sauvignon: Both are very similar, strong aromatic-

Ruby Cabernet: spicy aroma both in the grape and its wine. The aroma is compared to green olive or weed; (Cut grass, herbaceous).

Petite Sarah: Moderately distinctive with a difficult

odor to describe. It has a fruity ripe-grape character.

Pinot noir: It has one of the most difficult and elusive aromas to describe. The odor is strong unless the grapes are overripe. Its varietal aroma increases during the first few years of aging. It has been described as pepperminty.

Less and non-distinctive aromas

Carignane, Grenache, Gamay and Nebbiolo

Bouquet:

All young wines have a yeasty fermentation bouquet. This yeasty bouquet lasts less than a year. Most wines lose this yeasty odor within a few months of bottle aging. Wines made by maceration carbonique retain this musty bouquet longer. It is not found to be agreeable to everyone.

There are several other important odors imparted on wines during processing.

1) The baked bouquet of sherry or port (very distinct

caramel-like odor).

2) Sparkling wines which have been held on yeast

for extended periods of time, develop a very distinct bouquet,

3) Wines aged in wood (oak) add a desirable bouquet if not overdone.

Aging in the bottle often causes a special bouquet, especially in red wines. It is easier to recognize than is to describe. It is much more subtle than most of the other bouquets.

Foreign and Undesirable Odors:

One of the most serious problems with wines are foreign and undesirable odors. This includes off odors and odors that are not where they belong. For example, a recognizable woody odor in most white wines is a negative factor. Another example would be the baked odor of a sherry in a table wine is also highly undesirable.

A common undesirable odor in white wines is that of sulfur dioxide. Sulfur dioxide is the smell of a burning match. It is a negative quality and repulsive to most people. Sulfur dioxide is found in white wines of low pH. Besides being an undesirable quality, it masks desirable odors. In high concentrations, it can cause sneezing and pain. Detectable SO_2 odor is a sign of poor winemaking practice.

Most of the remaining undesirable odors can be categorized by their source. They are:

a) From the grapes,

b) Due to fermentation and or later processing, and

c) Due to microbial contamination.

Off-odors derived from the grape are earthy, green, raisiny, stemmy and moldy.

Earthiness is an off-odor found in specific areas. The earthy character is perceived after the wine has been in the mouth for a few seconds. Though commonly spoken of as an odor, is a mixed sensation and should be considered as a flavor. Tests have shown it is not from the soil or the grapes but is thought to be caused by particular localized micro flora on the grapes or perhaps on the winery equipment. The green or leafy odor is caused by identifiable compounds (6-carbon alcohols and aldehydes). Grapes grown in cool climates or immature grapes can produce wines with this off-odor. The raisiny odor is easily recognized as the caramel odor. It is caused by the use of raisined grapes for winemaking.

The odor stemminess has just about disappeared with the almost universal use of crusher-destemmers. It is easily identified by anyone who has crush grapes and has smelled discarded stems. It is an herbaceous, cut grass odor.

There are numerous undesirable odors caused by bad manufacturing practices during fermentation and processing of wine. These are baked, cooked, corked, fusel, hydrogen sulfide, mousy, oxidized, etc. The cooked odor is distinctly different from baked. It is caused by the wine being fermented at too high a temperature. This is still a prevalent problem throughout the world especially among white wines fermented above 25°C. The vast majority of commercial wineries have realized to make good white wine cooling is necessary.

Corked is an undesirable odor that develops just in wines sealed with corks. It is found in both new and old wines. It is found when porous corks are used. Most often, species of bacteria penetrate the pores of the cork and start decay of the cork. It is not common and without difficulty avoided. Bottles of wine suffering from this disorder have leaked through the cork. Therefore, avoid buying any wine that shows signs of leakage. This problem can be controlled by treating the corks with SO2 prior to their use. At home, one can make a solution of 100 ppm SO2 and soak the dry corks in the solution before using them to seal bottles of wine.

FUSEL ODOR IS AN EASILY identified odor and a more prevalent problem in dessert wines. It is caused by multiple carbon alcohols which are called fusel oils. At high concentrations, it is unpleasant, but in small dosages it adds character and complexity to a wine.

Hydrogen sulfide and mercaptans are detectable in minute amounts (two parts in a billion). It is the rotten egg smell. It is one of the most common foreign odors. They are produced from decaying yeast. The smell disappears after the first racking. There are several types of microorganisms that cause off-odors in wine. Most of them are wild yeast or bacteria. All these microorganisms attack organic compound in the wine, such as tartaric acid, alcohol, sugar, glycerin, etc. They cause off-odors. These off-odors indicate other serious chemical imbalances in the wine. The cause of the musty odor in some wines has not yet been isolated. However, it seems to be associated with bacterial growth (actinomycetes). The microbial origin of the mousy odor is also in question. It is associated with wines that have a high oxidation-reduction potential and oxidized wine.

Small amounts of acetic acid are produced by yeast during alcoholic fermentation. New wines range between O.02 to 0.03 gm of acetic acid/100 ml of wine. Higher concentrations result from contamination by one of the Acetobacter species. Acetic acid bacteria require large amounts of oxygen to grow and to oxidize ethanol to acetic acid. Acidification can be avoided by controlling the amount of air the wine is exposed to.

The other major microbial disorder wine suffer from is lactic acid bacteria. Lactic acid bacteria cause a common problem known as malo-lactic fermentation. The bacteria convert malic acid to lactic acid, thus reducing the total titratable acid and causes a butter-like aroma. In the past few years, there has been an effort to standardize the wine aroma terminology. The Sensory Evaluation Sub-committee of the American Society of Enology and Viticulture have proposed an interesting system. Their system is based on three levels of specificity from general to specific. The figure on the next page shows the three-tiered wheel of wine aroma terminology they proposed.

List of Wine Aroma Terminology

Taste

Taste in contrast to odor is limited today to 3 basic sensations; sour or acid, hitter and sweet. The sensation of taste is localized in special receptors on the tongue. Taste and flavor may begin together, but flavors are caused by compounds that once warmed up in the mouth. Their aromatic natures are detected by the olfactory nerve. It is simple to check by comparing the taste and flavor of a wine when your nose is tightly sealed during a normal tasting.

Sweetness

The two primary factors for sweetness are glucose and fructose (two reducing sugars) and to a limited extent by glycerol. These are modified by the alcohol content of a wine. Ethanol enhances the apparent sweetness while tannins reduce it. Fructose is the sweeter of the two sugars. Our ability to detect fructose is 35 to 50% greater than glucose, depending on their concentrations. For many people, sweetness masks or reduce the amount of sourness due to high acidity. Sweetness masks to some extent many other sensations such as astringency, bitterness and vinegary. The sugar in sweet wines helps to appease our appetite, thus reducing to some extent the enjoyment and requirement for food. Hunger in humans is a function of the amount of sugar in the blow stream. Dry table wines are preferred when eating a meal. It will thus add to our aesthetic pleasure of the food instead of reducing it

.

Bitterness

Most people find the taste of bitterness unpleasant. Bitterness is caused by tannins, flavonoids, and other compounds. This is because, white and rose wines have little tannin, and it is rare to find a bitter wine among them. However, full-bodied red wines are high in tannins and can have a bitter taste. Bitterness should not be confused with astringency. High astringency can mask bitter tastes. Not all bitterness is considered a negative trait. Some bitterness in red wines can be found to be a positive attribute.

Sourness

Sour taste is an essential and desirable part of the taste of wine. Wines lacking in acid have a flat taste. The acid sugar ratio in all fruit is Crucial to the taste. Any fruit which is lacking in sufficient acid will be flat in taste and this is considered a negative trait. The sourness of wine is a function of the total acidity and its pH. Sourness is affected by sweetness of the wine, a person's saliva, the buffering capacity of the wine and the balance of different organic acids present.

Wines that have a pH of less than 3.1 or total acidity of more than 0.9% will taste sour. Wines with a pH above 3.75 or with a total acidity less than 0.5% will taste flat. The terms tart, green or unripe are used to describe high acid (sour) wines.

Different acids, in equal amounts, cause varying degrees of sourness. Sourness of the basic four organic acids, found in wine, from the sourest to the least are tartaric>citric>malic>lactic. The appropriate amount of acidity in a wine depends on the type of wine. White wines like Rieslings should be rather high in acid while sourness in sweet dessert wines gives the wine an unpleasant sweet-sour taste.

Touch

The feel, touch or tactile sensations that wine gives us, are important characteristics, which allow us to appreciate more the wine. It is important that one can distinguish between the sensations of taste from feel. The two important features of the sensation of touch are astringency and viscosity. Astringency (puckery) is the sensation that causes our months and tongues to feel dried out. Astringency causes a stern, terse contraction or compression of soft organic tissue. It is a sensation of feeling to be distinguished from bitterness, which is a sensation of taste. Astringency in wines is caused by tannins (polyphenolic compounds). Astringency has a tendency to mask bitterness, and the amount of astringency in young wines decreases with aging. Viscosity is the amount or degree to which a liquid is fluid. The term 'body' is often used synonymously with viscosity. The more viscous a liquid the more body it has. The body or viscosity of a wine is due primarily to the ethanol and sugar content and only minimally by glycerol. Glycerol is a much more viscous compound, but it is found in low levels in wine.

It is an easy procedure to check for the body of a wine and its alcohol content. Fill a Clear wine glass 1/2-2/3 full with wine. Then swirl the wine around the glass and set it down. Above the present level of the wine, you will observe a small amount of wine dripping down the glass in tear shapes. The size and length of time it takes the tears to flow back into the main body of the wine indicates the viscosity of the wine. The larger the tears and the slower they move, the greater the viscosity and the higher the amount of alcohol.

Temperature

There are two reasons temperatures are important in the sensory evaluation of wines. First, the sensation of warm or cold in themselves are important. Second, the effect of temperature on our other senses, which can alternate our judgment of a wine. A warm white wine is found less pleasing than the same wine served cold, Sparkling wines also maintain their gassiness better when kept at low temperatures. Low temperatures also lower the volatility of compounds, which would make high SO_2 wines less repellant. Aromatic compounds will be more active and easier to identify when a wine is served warm.

There are as many systems for scoring wines as there are stars in the sky. Everyone has their particular system, some based on numerical values given for different characteristics and some based on verbal or written evaluation. I prefer and use the system of scoring developed in the University of California at Davis. It covers all the essential qualities of wine and leaves flexibility. This allows for subjective preferences to be included in the evaluation of the wine. This enables one to give values for a wine based on the general quality. Researchers found that concentrating only on the wines' characteristics do not add up a realistic picture of what the wine's true evaluation. This portion of the test enables one to round out the wine's quality. The system is based on numerical each characteristic. The total possible numerical score a wine can receive is 20 points, Wines with a score between 20 to 17 are superior wines.

Wines that have no outstanding merit or defect are scored 13 to 16. Wines having scores of 9 to 12 are wines with some defect, but still commercially acceptable scoring is given in the following manner:

Appearance: Cloudy=0, clear=1, brilliant=2

Color Distinctly off=0, slightly off=1, correct=2

Aroma & Bouquet Vinous=1, distinct, but not varietal=2, varietal=3

Vinegary Obvious=0, slight=1 none=2 Subtract 1 or 2 points for off- odors and add 1 for bottle bouquet.

Total Acidity Distinctly low or high=0, slightly low or high=1 correct=2

Sweetness Too high or low=0 correct=1

Body Too high or low=0 correct=1

Flavor Distinctly abnormal=0 slightly abnormal=1 correct=2

Bitterness Distinctly high=0 slightly high=1 correct=2

General Quality Lacking=0 slight=1 impressive =2

XI. SANITATION

Sanitation is not the same thing as cleaning or sterilization. To sanitize something is to reduce or remove bacteria and other undesirable microorganisms via heat or chemical means. Cleaning is the removal of visible dirt and residue from your equipment. Sterilization is the killing of germs, insects, or worms.

If your latest attempt at winemaking was less than satisfactory, then look no further than the area in which you made your wine. It is known that 90% of winemaking failures can be traced back to poor standards of sanitation of the equipment or/and the area of the production.

Sanitation plays an important role in winemaking. It is important for the quality of the wine and for the health of the people making the wine. All the equipment used in winemaking should be kept clean to prevent microbial contamination and off tastes, aromas, and flavors. Before any equipment is used, it should be checked to see if it is absolutely clean. Foreign materials can attribute to the reduction of the quality of the wine or worst be toxic. Clean all equipment well and use plenty of water to wash away any residue of the cleaning agents.

The area in which you work should also be kept clean to prevent accidents (such as slipping on wet garbage left around) and to prevent microbial contamination. There should always be a good source of water close at hand for cleaning up. Garbage disposal is also important. Moldy unused grapes, pumice or less left around will attract insects and possibility rodents. Always have garbage pails and bags available for immediate clean up.

Sanitation during bottling is important to prevent spoilage in the bottle. To finish all this long process and then have the wine spoil in the bottle would be a real shame. Treat the corks with SO2 before use and clean the bottles with proper cleaning agents. Use sterile boiled water (boil the water for 20 minutes) to make the final rinse of the bottles before filling. This should be done immediately before bottling to ensure that the bottles are as clean as possible.

Below is a table providing a partial list of the different cleaning and disinfecting agents that can be used.

Cleaning and Disinfecting Agents

A. Cleaning agents for plastic or glassware

1. Boiling water
2. Tri-sodium phosphate
3. Potassium Meta-bi-sulfite
4. Soda Ash
5. Hydrogen peroxide

A. For cleaning wood or concrete

1. Tri-sodium phosphate
2. Sodium bicarbonate
3. Soda Ash
4. Boiling water
5. Chlorine
6. Hydrogen peroxide

A. For Metal Equipment

1. Any of the materials for cleaning wood
2. Citric Acid
3. Abrasive carbon

A. For Sterilizing

1. Sodium or calcium hypochlorite
2. Sulfur dioxide

A. For Outside- Wood or Concrete

1. Lime

2.   Sodium or calcium hypochlorite
3.   Sodium Bisulfate

After the use of any of these cleaning agents, the equipment must be rinsed thoroughly with plenty of water.

The last step in our long procedure is to raise a glass "To Your Health".

List of Aroma and Taste Terminology

———

Taste in contrast to odor is limited to 3 basic sensations: sour or acid, bitter and sweet. The sensation of taste is localized in special receptors on our tongues. Taste and flavor may begin together, but flavors are caused by compounds that once warmed up in the mouth, their aromatic natures are detected by the olfactory nerve (smell). This can be easily checked by comparing the taste and flavor of a wine when your nose is tightly sealed to a normal tasting.

The two primary factors for sweetness are glucose and fructose (both reducing sugars) and to a limited extent by glycerol. These are modified by the alcohol content of the wine. Ethanol enhances the apparent sweetness while tannins reduce it. Fructose is the sweeter of the two sugars. Our ability to detect fructose is 35-50% greater than glucose, depending on their concentrations. For many people, sweetness masks or reduce the amount of sourness due to high acidity. Sweetness masks to some extent, many other sensations; such as astringency, bitterness and vinegary. The sugar in sweet wines helps to appease our appetite, thus reducing to some extent the amount of sugar in the blood stream. Dry table wines are preferred when eating a meal. It will thus add to our aesthetic pleasure of the food instead of reducing it.

Acetic: All wines, contain amounts of acidity due to acetic acid. It is what gives it the vinegary smell. In excessive amounts, the wine will have a vinegary smell, essential wine vinegar.

Acidic: Wines need natural acidity[1] to taste fresh[2] and lively. Excessive amounts of acidity results in a wine that is tart[3] and sour.

Acidity: A proper acid balance in a wine is critical to its quality. It is the nature of wine to contain citric, tartaric, malic, and lactic acids. Wines made from

---

1. https://www.erobertparker.com/info/glossary.asp#acidity

2. https://www.erobertparker.com/info/glossary.asp#fresh

3. https://www.erobertparker.com/info/glossary.asp#tart

grapes from hot areas are lower in acidity, whereas wines from cool to moderate temperatures are higher in acidity. Acidity in a wine can preserve the wine's freshness and keep the wine lively, but too much acidity will mask the wines flavors and compresses its texture.

Aftertaste: The taste left in one's mouth swallowing the wine is the aftertaste. It is a synonym for length or finish. The longer the aftertaste lingers in the mouth, the higher the quality of the wine.

Aggressive: Aggressive applies to wines that are high in acidity or harsh[4] tannins or both.

Aroma: Aroma is the smell of a young wine before it has had sufficient time to develop nuances of smell that are then called its bouquet[5]. The word aroma is used to mean the smell of a relatively young, unevolved wine.

Astringent: Wines that are astringent are not necessarily bad or good wines. Astringent wines are harsh[6] and coarse to taste, because they are too young and tannic[7] and just need time to develop, or because they are not well made. The level of tannins (if it is harsh) in a wine contributes to its degree of astringency. It is the sensation you mouth is dried out or pucker, like after eating an unripe persimmon.

Balance: One of the most desired characteristics in a wine is to have good balance. That is where the concentration of fruit, level of tannins, and acidity[8] are in total harmony. Balanced wines are symmetrical and improve with age.

Berrylike: Most red wines have an intense berry fruit character that can suggest blackberries, raspberries, black cherries, mulberries, or even strawberries and cranberries.

---

4. https://www.erobertparker.com/info/glossary.asp#harsh

5. https://www.erobertparker.com/info/glossary.asp#bouquet

6. https://www.erobertparker.com/info/glossary.asp#harsh

7. https://www.erobertparker.com/info/glossary.asp#tannic

8. https://www.erobertparker.com/info/glossary.asp#acidity

Bitterness: Most people find the taste of bitterness unpleasant. Bitterness is caused by tannins, flavonoids, and other organic compounds. Since white and rose wines have little tannin, it is rare to find a bitter wine among them. However, full-bodied red wines are high in tannins and can have a bitter taste. Bitterness should not be confused with astringency.

Blackcurrant: A pronounced smell of blackcurrant fruit. It can vary in intensity from faint to deep and rich.

Body: Body is the weight or viscosity of a wine that can be sensed as it crosses the palate. It is expressed as full-bodied, medium-bodied or medium-weight, or light-bodied. It is an easy procedure to check the body and alcohol content of a wine. Fill a clear wine glass 1/2 to 2/3rds full with wine. Then swirl the wine around the glass and set it down. Above the present level of the wine, you will observe a small amount of wine dripping down the glass in tear shaped structures. The size and length of time it takes the tears to flow back into the main body of the wine indicates the viscosity of the wine. The larger the tears and the slower they move, the greater the viscosity and the higher the amount of alcohol.

Botrytis cinerea: This fungus attacks the grape skins under specific climatic conditions (moist and warm weather). It causes the grape to become super-concentrated because it causes a natural dehydration. Botrytis cinerea is essential for the great sweet white wines of Barsac and Sauternes.

Bouquet: As a wine's aroma[9] becomes more developed from bottle aging, the aroma is transformed into a bouquet[10] that is hopefully more than just the smell of the grape.

Brawny: A full-bodied[11] wine with plenty of weight and flavor, although not always the most elegant[12] or refined sort of wine.

---

9. https://www.erobertparker.com/info/glossary.asp#aroma

10. https://www.erobertparker.com/info/glossary.asp#bouquet

11. https://www.erobertparker.com/info/glossary.asp#full-bodied

12. https://www.erobertparker.com/info/glossary.asp#elegant

Briery: One thinks of California Zinfandel when the term briery comes into play, denoting that the wine is aggressive[13] and rather spicy[14].

Brilliant: Brilliant relates to the color of the wine. A brilliant wine is one that is clear, with no haze or cloudiness to the color.

Browning: As red wines age, their color changes from ruby/purple to dark ruby, to medium ruby, to ruby with an amber edge, to ruby with a brown edge. When a wine is browning, it is mature and will not improve any more.

Cedar: Reds wines can have a bouquet[15] that suggests either faintly or overtly the smell of cedar wood. It is a complex aspect of the bouquet.

Chewy: If a wine has a rather dense, viscous[16] texture from a high glycerin content, it is often referred to as being chewy. High-extract[17] wines from great vintages can often be chewy, because they have higher alcohol hence high levels of glycerin, which imparts a fleshy[18] mouth feel.

Closed: The term closed is used to denote that the wine is not showing its potential, which remains locked in because it is too young. Young wines often close up about 12-18 months after bottling and depending on the vintage and storage conditions, remain in such a state for several years to more than a decade.

Complex: One of the most subjective descriptive terms used, a complex wine is a wine that the taster never gets bored with and finds interesting to drink. Complex wines have a variety of subtle scents and flavors that hold one's interest in the wine.

Concentrated: Fine wines, whether they are light-, medium-, or full-bodied[19], should have concentrated flavors. Concentrated denotes that the wine has a

---

13. https://www.erobertparker.com/info/glossary.asp#aggressive

14. https://www.erobertparker.com/info/glossary.asp#spicy

15. https://www.erobertparker.com/info/glossary.asp#bouquet

16. https://www.erobertparker.com/info/glossary.asp#viscous

17. https://www.erobertparker.com/info/glossary.asp#extract

18. https://www.erobertparker.com/info/glossary.asp#fleshy

depth and richness of fruit that gives it appeal and interest. Deep[20] is a synonym for concentrated.

Corked: A corked wine is a flawed wine that has taken on the smell of cork because of an unclean or faulty cork. It has a smell similar to wet cardboard.

Cuvée: Many producers in the Rhône Valley produce special, deluxe lots of wine or a lot of wine from a specific grape variety they bottle separately. These lots are often referred to as cuvées.

Deep: Essentially the same as concentrated[21], indicating the wine is rich[22], full of extract[23], and mouth filling.

Delicate: As this word implies, delicate wines are light, subtle, understated wines that are prized for their shyness rather than for an extroverted, robust character. White wines are more delicate than red wines. Few Rhône red wines can correctly be called delicate.

Diffuse: Wines that smell and taste unstructured and unfocused are said to be diffuse. When red wines are served at too warm a temperature, they often become diffuse.

Earthy: May be used in both a negative and a positive sense; however, I prefer to use earthy to denote a positive aroma[24] of fresh, rich, clean soil. Earthy is a more intense smell than woody[25] or truffle scents.

Elegant: Although more white wines than red are described as being elegant, lighter-styled, graceful, balance[26] red wines can be elegant.

---

19. https://www.erobertparker.com/info/glossary.asp#full-bodied

20. https://www.erobertparker.com/info/glossary.asp#Deep

21. https://www.erobertparker.com/info/glossary.asp#concentrated

22. https://www.erobertparker.com/info/glossary.asp#rich

23. https://www.erobertparker.com/info/glossary.asp#extract

24. https://www.erobertparker.com/info/glossary.asp#aroma

25. https://www.erobertparker.com/info/glossary.asp#woody

26. https://www.erobertparker.com/info/glossary.asp#balance

Exuberant: Like extroverted, somewhat hyper people, wines too can gush with fruit and seem nervous and intensely vigorous.

Floral: Wines made from the Muscat grapes have a flowery component, and occasionally a red wine will have a floral scent.

Focused: Both of a fine wine's bouquet[27] and flavor should be focused. Focused means that the scents, aromas, and flavors are precise and clearly delineated. If they are not, the wine is like an out-of-focus picture-diffuse[28], hazy, and problematic.

Forward: An adjective used to describe wines that are (1) delicious, evolved, and close to maturity, (2) wines that border on being flamboyant or ostentatious, or (3) unusually evolved and/or quickly maturing wines.

Fresh: Freshness in both young and old wines is a welcome and pleasing component. A wine is said to be fresh when it is lively and cleanly made. The opposite of fresh is stale[29].

Fruity: A superb wine should have enough concentration of fruit so it can be said to be fruity. The best wines will have more than just a fruity personality.

Full-bodied: Wines rich in extract[30], alcohol, and glycerin are full-bodied wines.

Green: Green wines are wines made from under ripe grapes; they lack taste and aroma of their varietal[31] character.

Hard: Hard wines have abrasive, astringent[32] tannins or high acidity[33]. Young vintages of red wines can be hard, but they should never be harsh[34].

---

27. https://www.erobertparker.com/info/glossary.asp#bouquet

28. https://www.erobertparker.com/info/glossary.asp#diffuse

29. https://www.erobertparker.com/info/glossary.asp#stale

30. https://www.erobertparker.com/info/glossary.asp#extract

31. https://www.erobertparker.com/info/glossary.asp#vegetal

32. https://www.erobertparker.com/info/glossary.asp#astringent

33. https://www.erobertparker.com/info/glossary.asp#acidity

Harsh: If a wine is too hard it is said to be harsh. Harshness in a wine, young or old, is a flaw.

Herbaceous: Many wines have a distinctive herbal smell that is said to be herbaceous. Specific herbal smells can be of thyme, lavender, rosemary, oregano, fennel, or basil. Cabernet Sauvignon has a distinct herbaceous taste when they are young.

Hollow: Also known as shallow, hollow wines are diluted and lack depth and concentration.

Hot: Rather than meaning that the temperature of the wine is too warm to drink, hot denotes that the wine is too high in alcohol and, therefore, leaves a burning sensation in the back of the throat when swallowed. Wines with alcohol levels over 14.5% often taste hot if the requisite depth of fruit is not present.

Intensity: Intensity is one of the most desirable traits of a high-quality wine. Wines of great intensity must also have balance[35]. They should never be heavy or cloying. Intensely concentrated[36] great wines are alive, vibrant, aromatic, layered, and texturally compelling. Their intensity adds to their character, rather than detracting from it.

Leafy: A leafy character in a wine is similar to a herbaceous[37] character; because it refers to the smell of leaves rather than herbs. A wine that is too leafy is a vegetal[38] or green[39] wine.

Lean: Lean wines are slim, rather streamlined wines that lack generosity and fatness but can still be enjoyable and pleasant.

---

34. https://www.erobertparker.com/info/glossary.asp#harsh

35. https://www.erobertparker.com/info/glossary.asp#balance

36. https://www.erobertparker.com/info/glossary.asp#concentrated

37. https://www.erobertparker.com/info/glossary.asp#herbaceous

38. https://www.erobertparker.com/info/glossary.asp#vegetal

39. https://www.erobertparker.com/info/glossary.asp#green

Lively: A synonym for fresh[40] or exuberant[41], a lively wine is usually young wine with good acidity[42] and a thirst-quenching personality.

Long: a desirable trait in any fine wine is that it be long in the mouth. Long (or length) relates to a wine's finish, meaning that after you swallow the wine, you sense its presence for a long time. (Thirty seconds to several minutes is great length.) In a young wine, the difference between something good and something great is the length of the wine.

Lush: Lush wines are velvety[43], soft[44], richly fruity wines that are both concentrated[45] and fat[46]. A lush wine can never be an astringent[47] or hard[48] wine.

Musty: Wines aged in dirty barrels or unwept cellars or exposed to a bad cork take on a damp, musty character that is a flaw.

Nose: The general smell and aroma[49] of a wine as sensed through one's nose and olfactory senses is often called the wine's nose.

Oaky: Many red wines are aged from 6 months to 30 months in various sizes of oak barrels. New oak barrels impart a toasty[50], vanillin flavor and smell to the wine. If the wine is not rich[51] and concentrated[52], the barrels can overwhelm the wine, making it taste overly oaky. Where the wine is rich and concentrated

---

40. https://www.erobertparker.com/info/glossary.asp#fresh

41. https://www.erobertparker.com/info/glossary.asp#exuberant

42. https://www.erobertparker.com/info/glossary.asp#acidity

43. https://www.erobertparker.com/info/glossary.asp#velvety

44. https://www.erobertparker.com/info/glossary.asp#soft

45. https://www.erobertparker.com/info/glossary.asp#concentrated

46. https://www.erobertparker.com/info/glossary.asp#fat

47. https://www.erobertparker.com/info/glossary.asp#astringent

48. https://www.erobertparker.com/info/glossary.asp#hard

49. https://www.erobertparker.com/info/glossary.asp#aroma

50. https://www.erobertparker.com/info/glossary.asp#toasty

51. https://www.erobertparker.com/info/glossary.asp#rich

52. https://www.erobertparker.com/info/glossary.asp#concentrated

and the winemaker has made a judicious use of barrels, however, the results are a wonderful marriage of fruit and oak.

Off: If a wine is not showing its true character or is flawed or spoiled it is said to be "off."

Overripe: An undesirable characteristic from grapes left too long on the vine that became too ripe. They lose their acidity[53], and produce wines that are heavy and balance[54]. This can happen in the hot viticultural areas, if the growers harvest too late.

Oxidized: If a wine has been excessively exposed to air during either its making or aging, the wine loses freshness and takes on a stale[55], old smell, and taste. Such a wine is said to be oxidized.

Perfumed: This term is more applicable to fragrant, aromatic white wines than to red wines. However, some dry white wines (particularly Condrieu) and sweet white wines can have a strong perfumed smell.

Plummy: Rich[56], concentrated[57] wines can often have the smell and taste of ripe plums. When they do, the term plummy applies.

Precocious: Wines that mature quickly are precocious. However, the term also applies to wines that may last and evolve gracefully over a long period, but taste as if they are aging quickly because of their tastiness and soft[58], early charms.

Raisin-like: Late-harvest wines that are drunk at the end of a meal can often have a somewhat raisin-like flavor, which in some ports and Sherries is desirable. However, a raisin-like quality is a major flaw in a dinner wine.

Rich: Wines high in extract[59], flavor, and intensity[60] of fruit flavor.

---

53. https://www.erobertparker.com/info/glossary.asp#acidity

54. https://www.erobertparker.com/info/glossary.asp#balance

55. https://www.erobertparker.com/info/glossary.asp#stale

56. https://www.erobertparker.com/info/glossary.asp#rich

57. https://www.erobertparker.com/info/glossary.asp#concentrated

58. https://www.erobertparker.com/info/glossary.asp#soft

59. https://www.erobertparker.com/info/glossary.asp#extract

Ripe: A wine is ripe when its grapes have reached the optimum level of maturity. Immature grapes produce wines are under ripe, and over mature grapes produce wines that are overripe[61].

Round: A desirable character of wines, roundness occurs in mature wines that have lost their youthful, astringent[62] tannins, and also in young wines that have soft[63] tannins and low acidity[64].

Shallow: A weak, feeble, watery or diluted wine lacking concentration is said to be shallow.

Sharp: An undesirable trait, sharp wines are bitter and unpleasant with hard[65], pointed edges.

silky: A synonym for velvety[66] or lush[67], silky wines are soft[68], sometimes fat[69], but never hard[70] or angular[71].

Smoky: Some wines, because of the soil or because of the barrels used to age the wine, have a distinctive smoky character

Soft: A soft wine is round[72] and fruity, low in acidity[73], and has an absence of aggressive[74], hard[75] tannins.

---

60. https://www.erobertparker.com/info/glossary.asp#intensity

61. https://www.erobertparker.com/info/glossary.asp#overripe

62. https://www.erobertparker.com/info/glossary.asp#astringent

63. https://www.erobertparker.com/info/glossary.asp#soft

64. https://www.erobertparker.com/info/glossary.asp#acidity

65. https://www.erobertparker.com/info/glossary.asp#hard

66. https://www.erobertparker.com/info/glossary.asp#velvety

67. https://www.erobertparker.com/info/glossary.asp#lush

68. https://www.erobertparker.com/info/glossary.asp#soft

69. https://www.erobertparker.com/info/glossary.asp#fat

70. https://www.erobertparker.com/info/glossary.asp#hard

71. https://www.erobertparker.com/info/glossary.asp#angular

72. https://www.erobertparker.com/info/glossary.asp#round

73. https://www.erobertparker.com/info/glossary.asp#acidity

74. https://www.erobertparker.com/info/glossary.asp#aggressive

Sourness: The sour taste is an essential and desirable component of the taste of a wine. The lack of acid in wines, cause them to have a flat taste. The acid: sugar ratio in all fruits is crucial to the taste. Any fruit which is lacking in sufficient acid will be flat in taste and it is considered a negative trait. The sourness of a wine is a function of the total acidity and its pH. Wines that have a pH of less than 3.1 or total acidity of more than 0.9% will taste sour. Wines with a pH above 3.75 or a total acidity less than 0.5% will taste flat (insipid). The term tart, green or unripe are used to describe high acid (sour) wines.

Spicy: Wines often smell spicy with aromas of pepper, cinnamon, and other well-known spices. These pungent aromas are lumped together and called spicy.

Supple: A supple wine is one that is soft[76], lush[77], velvety[78], round[79] and tasty. It is a desirable characteristic because it suggests that the wine is harmonious.

Tannic: The tannins of a wine are extracted from the grape skins and stems. Along with a wine's acidity[80] and alcohol, tannin is an essential part of the wine's history. Tannins give a wine firmness and some roughness when young, but the roughness dissipates with time. A tannic wine is one that is young and unready to drink.

Tart: Sharp[81], acidic[82], under aged wines are called tart. A wine that is tart is not pleasant to drink.

Temperature: There are two reasons temperature is important in the sensory evaluation of wines. First, the sensation of warm or cold in themselves, and second, the effect of temperature on the other senses, which might influence our judgment. A warm white wine is found less pleasing than the same wine

---

75. https://www.erobertparker.com/info/glossary.asp#hard

76. https://www.erobertparker.com/info/glossary.asp#soft

77. https://www.erobertparker.com/info/glossary.asp#lush

78. https://www.erobertparker.com/info/glossary.asp#velvety

79. https://www.erobertparker.com/info/glossary.asp#round

80. https://www.erobertparker.com/info/glossary.asp#acidity

81. https://www.erobertparker.com/info/glossary.asp#Sharp

82. https://www.erobertparker.com/info/glossary.asp#acidic

served cold. Sparkling wines also maintain their gassiness better when kept at low temperatures. Low temperatures also lower the volatility of compounds. This would make high SO2 wines less repellant. Aromatic compounds will be more active and easier to recognize, when a wine is served warm.

Velvety: A textural description and synonym for lush[83] or silky[84], a velvety wine is a rich[85], soft[86], smooth wine to taste. It is a desirable characteristic.

Viscous: Viscous wines are concentrated[87], fat[88], almost thick[89] wines with a great density of fruit extract[90], plenty of glycerin, and high alcohol content. If they have balancing acidity[91], they can be flavorful and exciting wines. If they lack acidity, they are often flabby[92] and heavy.

Volatile: A volatile wine is one that smells of vinegar because of an excessive amount of acetic[93] bacteria present. It is a seriously flawed wine.

Woody: When a wine is overly oaky[94] it is often said to be woody. Oakiness in a wine's bouquet[95] and taste is good up to a point. Once past that point, the wine is woody and its fruity qualities are masked by excessive oak aging.

---

83. https://www.erobertparker.com/info/glossary.asp#lush

84. https://www.erobertparker.com/info/glossary.asp#silky

85. https://www.erobertparker.com/info/glossary.asp#rich

86. https://www.erobertparker.com/info/glossary.asp#soft

87. https://www.erobertparker.com/info/glossary.asp#concentrated

88. https://www.erobertparker.com/info/glossary.asp#fat

89. https://www.erobertparker.com/info/glossary.asp#thick

90. https://www.erobertparker.com/info/glossary.asp#extract

91. https://www.erobertparker.com/info/glossary.asp#acidity

92. https://www.erobertparker.com/info/glossary.asp#flabby

93. https://www.erobertparker.com/info/glossary.asp#acetic

94. https://www.erobertparker.com/info/glossary.asp#oaky

95. https://www.erobertparker.com/info/glossary.asp#bouquet

Below is the popular wine aroma wheel developed at the University of California at Davis. Figure 13. Aroma Wheel.

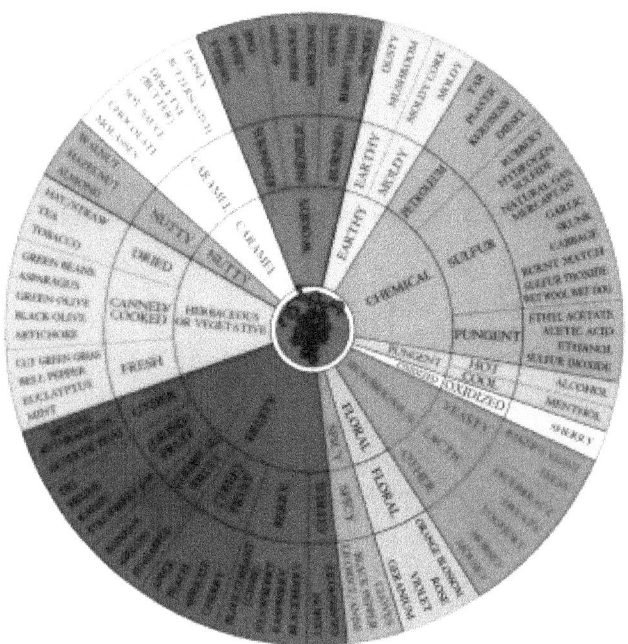

APPENDIX I

LIST OF WINE ADDITIVES

ACTIVATED CHARCOAL: To assist precipitation during fermentation to clarify wine. To remove excess color in white wines.

Bentonite: To clarify wine

Calcium Carbonate: To reduce excess acid

Casein: To clarify wine

Di-ammonium Hydrogen

Phosphate (NH4) 2HPO4: Yeast food to aid in difficult fermentation products (like fruit and honey wine)

Egg whites: To clarify wines

Fumaric acid: Antiseptic, to prevent malo-lactic fermentation. It also adds to the total acidity

Gum Arabic: To clarify and stabilize wine.

Lactic acid: To add acid to fruit wines

Malic acid: To increase total acidity of wine

Nitrogen gas: To prevent oxidation, to maintain pressure during filtering and bottling of sparkling wines.

Oak chips: To simulate aging in oak barrels.

Potassium (or Sodium) meta-bisulfate to prevent oxidation antiseptic to kill wild yeast before initiation of fermentation.

Sorbic acid: antiseptic and preservative, to inhibit

malo-lactic fermentation.

Tannin: To aid in the clarification of wine.

Tartaric acid: To increase the total acidity of wine.

APPENDIX II

List of Equipment and Chemicals

Fermenting and Processing

1. Airlocks

2. Bottles-many of all sizes

3. Crushing vat

Wood, stainless steel, plastic

4. Fermenting Vessels

Glass jars, food-grade plastic containers, stainless steel,

Water-proof wood barrels

5. Funnels

6. Hosing, tubing

Polyethylene, Teflon, silicon, stainless steel

7. Hydrometer

8. Press

Gauze cloth, mechanical

9, Refractometer

10. Stick for mixing cap

11. Thermometer

Wine and Must Analysis

1. pH-Litmus paper

2. Sugar -refractometer or hydrometer

3. Kit for testing for total acid

Fining and Clarifying Agents

1. Bentonite

2. Casein

3. Egg whites

4. gelatin

5. Charcoal

Bottling

1. Bottling

2. Corks

3. Corking device

4. Seals

Sanitation

1. Antiseptic-SO_2

2. Detergent

3. Garbage pails and bags

4. Soda Ash

5. Sodium meta-bisulfate

6. Sodium Carbonate

7. Sodium hypochlorite (bleach)

8. Water hose.

REFERENCES

Amerine M. A., W. Berg; and W. V. Cruess. Technology of Wine Making. 1972. Avi Publishing, Westport. Conn.

Amerine M. A., W. V. Cruess, H. W. Berg; R. E. Kunkee, C. S. Ough, V. L. Singleton, and A. D. Webb. Table Wines and Dessert and Appetizer Wines Technology of Winemaking 1967, Avi Publishing, Westport. Conn.

Amerine M. A. and M.A. Joslyn. Table Wines: The Technology of their Production. 1973. University of California Press, Berkeley.

Amerine M. A. and C. S. Ough, Wine and Must Analysis. 1974. John Wiley and Sons. Canada

Amerine, M.A. and E. B. Roessler Wines: Their Sensory Evaluation, 1983 (W.H. Freeman & Company).

Amerine, M.A. and V. L. Singleton. Wine, An Introduction. Revised edition 1975. University of California Press, Berkley.

Boulton, R.B., V.L. Singleton, L.F. Bisson, and R.E. Kunkee. Principles and Practices of Winemaking. 1996 Chapman & Hall (International Thomson Publishing). New York:

Crues, W.V., M.A. Joslyn, L.G. Swell. Laboratory Examination of Wines and other Fermented Fruit Products. 1934, Avi Publishing Co. New York.

Dharmadhikari. M., Composition of Grapes 2019. https://www.extension.iastate.edu/wine/wp-content/uploads/2021/09/compositionofgrapes.pdf

Frazier, N.W., J. P. Fulton, J.M. Thresh, R. H. Converse, E.H. Varney, and W. B. Hewitt. Virus Diseases of Small Fruits and Grapevines. 1970, University of California Press. Berkeley.

Irwin, J. Guide to Making Homemade Wine. 1992, Tiger Books International. London.

Johnson, H. Wine Companion 1987, Mitchell Beazley Intern. Ltd. London.

Johnson, H. Vintage: The Story of Wine. 198, Simon and Schuster. New York.

Johnson, H. and James Halliday. The Vintner's Art: How Great Wines are Made. 1992. Simon and Schuster. New York.

Kasimatis, A. N., B.E. Bearden, and K. Bowers. Wine Grape Varieties in the North Coast Counties of California. 1977 University of California Press. Berkeley.

Margalit, Y. Winery Technology & Operations: a Handbook for Small Wineries. 1996: The Wine Appreciation Guild. San Francisco.

Montefiore, A. Wine Talk: Ancient wine. 2012. http://www.jpost.com/Arts-and-Culture/Food-And-Wine/ Wine-Talk-Ancient-wine

Muscatine, D., Amerine, M. A. Thompson, B[1]., The Book of California Wine. 1984 University of California Press, Berkeley.

Olmo, H.P. 1948, Ruby Cabernet and Emerald Riesling. Calif. Agr. Exper. Stat. Bull. 704:1-12.

---

1. http://www.abebooks.com/servlet/

SearchResults?an=Muscatine%2C+Doris%3B+Amerine%2C+Maynard+A.%3B+Thompson%2C+Bob& cm_sp=det-_-bdp-_-author

Ough, C.S. and M.A. Amerine 1967. Studies with controlled fermentation. X. Effect of fermentation temperature on some volatile compounds in wine. Am. J. Enology & Viticulture. 18: 157-164.

Peynaud, E. The Taste of Wine: The Art and Science of Wine Appreciation. 1987. Macdonald & Co. (Publishers) Ltd. London

Robinson, J. Vines, Grapes, Wines. 1986, Mitchell Beazley. London.

Robinson, J., (ed.) The Oxford Companion to Wine – third edition. 2006. Oxford University Press. Oxford

Storm, J. An Introduction to Wines. 1955. Simon and Schuster. New York.

Webb, D.A, and H.W. Berg, Terms used in tasting. 1955. Wines and Vines (36 (7) 25-28.

Wein, B. Wine, http://www.rabbiwein.com/blog/wine-529.html

ABOUT THE AUTHOR

Dr. Barry Nadel was born in Texas (July 11, 1953), and grew up in San Jose, California (before it was Silicon Valley, in a traditional home that was Shomer Shabbat and kashrut. From 1971 to 1973 he studied Archaeology and Anthropology and switched to Enology and Viticulture, receiving his B.Sc. from UC Davis (1975) and his M.Sc. in grape genetics in 1977. He was the first person to do grape tissue culture at UC Davis. In 1976 he won the Winkler Scholarship from the Dept. of Viticulture and Enology.

That same summer he made aliyah to Israel to do his PhD in plant genetics at the Faculty of Agriculture, Hebrew University in Rehovot, which he received in 1981.

Dr. Nadel worked as a researcher in plant biotechnology and physiology for 6 years at the Faculty of Agriculture. He founded his own small vegetable seed company for 22 years, responsible for plant breeding, stock seed maintenance and seed production.

He served in the Army reserves for 13 years in the artillery (3 years in Lebanon, and 5 years of Intifada). Later, he was a full-time volunteer for the Border Police, responsible for the security of Moshav Kfar Pines for 10 years.

In 2002 he remarried to Hadassah, from Manchester, England, the love of his life. With her he reached the spiritual heights of selfless love with no thought of compensation. She died in his arms July 20, 2004 of cancer.

Dr. Nadel is currently chief scientist for a consortium medicinal Cannabis responsible for tissue culture, biotechnical research and plant breeding.

Dr. Nadel has three daughters, one son and eleven grandchildren (6 girls and 5 boys). He is both divorced and a widower. He has been writing for over 35 years both scientific and non-fiction works. For the past 30 years, Dr. Nadel has been writing fiction. In 2013 he decided to publish the fiction project called the Hoshiyan Chronicles. It is a highly spiritual work based on the principles of justice, Righteousness and Faith (www.drbnadel.com).

OTHER BOOKS

by Dr. Barry Nadel

Enjoy other books by Dr. Barry Nadel:

Non-Fiction

Art of Kosher Wine Making

Production of Medicinal Cannabis in Greenhouses

Spice and Herb Production in Greenhouses

Vegetable Production in Greenhouses

Greenhouse Setup Manual

Fiction The Hoshiyan Chronicles

Seeking the Light of Justice

Saving the Light of Justice

Oath of Peace

Forging the Light of Justice

Prophecy of the Light of Justice

NIA, farmer, scholar, prince

Mysterious Birth of the Light of Justice

Forging of a Spiritual Warrior

Forged in Fire

Light of Justice: Evolution of Leadership

Light of Justice: Spiritual Spy

Brewing Storm

Worthy of Love

Ultimate Treason.

https://books2read.com/ap/8V4VBy/Barry-Nadel